Psychologically Speaking
A Self-Assessment

Craig Poulenez Donovan
Peter C. Rosato
Kean College of New Jersey

Allyn and Bacon
Boston · London · Toronto · Sydney · Tokyo · Singapore

A Viacom Company
160 Gould Street
Needham Heights, Massachusetts 02194

Internet: www.abacon.com
America Online: keyword: College Online

ISBN 0-205-16364-5

Printed in the United States of America

10 9 8 7 6 5 4 3 2 1 00 99 98 97 96

TABLE OF CONTENTS

Section 6 INTELLIGENCE AND CREATIVITY

Section 7 HUMAN DEVELOPMENT

Section 8 MOTIVATION AND EMOTION

Section 9 CONSCIOUSNESS

Section 10 PERSONALITY

Section 11 PSYCHOLOGICAL DISORDERS

Section 12 TREATMENT AND THERAPY

Section 13 SOCIAL ASPECTS OF PSYCHOLOGY

Section 14 STRESS AND HEALTH

Section 15 PSYCHOLOGY IN THE WORKPLACE

A NOTE TO THE INSTRUCTOR

When this project was begun several years ago, it started out with the question, "What would help us to get our students more involved in the course while also helping them to learn?" Over time, we found that our students (just like ourselves) greatly enjoyed taking self-assessment style exams, hence their great popularity in the everyday press. Over time we began collecting those exams that met our criteria for ease of use, quality of learning material, and fun quotient.

Psychologically Speaking: A Self-Assessment was created and designed to serve as a supplement to any current introductory or self/adjustment psychology textbook, a supplement that may be kept and used for years to come even by non-psych majors. The exercises in *Psychologically Speaking* exist to help students begin to explore their knowledge and feelings about the field of psychology and their own role in the study of the mind. These exercises can either be done in or out of your classroom. They should serve to prompt reflection and discussion on a variety of personal and professional topics leading on to and supporting those used by you in the class.

We have used these exercises on our own students over the years. The feedback has been positive as has the learning experiences the students themselves underwent. In general, we try to provide the students ample time to complete each exercise. For some items this may mean assigning the exercise a few days before the class. For others we may typically take the first half of a class to complete the exercise and the second half to compare the results, first in small groups and then among the class as a whole.

Many of the exercises can be used in an additional way as a benchmark of learning over the course of the quarter/semester. These can be given in a pre and post class fashion (we especially recommend using 1.2 and 1.4 at the start and end of the course). With feedback to the students this can provide a direct and yet non-threatening way of measuring their growth and achievements over time. Although a good case could be made for using only items which had an extensive and rigid research pedigree, our use of these items over time has shown us that it is the ability of an exercise to stimulate and engage that is of greatest importance, not the number of academic citations that accompany them.

There are of course as many ways to organize a book as there are people who read. Clearly certain exercises could have been located in other sections and the sections themselves could have appeared in different orders of presentation. Some people might even argue for no sections per se. It is our belief that the book is more useful in having sections which match up to the topics covered in most introductory texts and we feel certain that each instructor who uses this book will have their own personal preference for which items to use in what order within their own classes.

The Many who can, do. The Few who understand, teach.
Proverb

A NOTE TO THE READERS AND/OR STUDENTS

Psychologically Speaking: A Self-Assessment has been created with you in mind. There are thousands of different psychological tests around us all today. We encounter them everyplace from the job interview to the magazine counter at the supermarket. They are used to determine what we should study, what jobs we should and should not get, who we might fall in love with, as well as to examine the innermost recesses of our personal selves.

Psychology itself is a central theme in life. Success in the world requires our ability to be able to understand and get along with our fellow men and women. Understanding ourselves better and better is the first step. Our goal here is, therefore, not to overwhelm you with a barrage of names, dates, and theories per se. Instead, we are trying to provide you with a series of tools to explore and expand your knowledge of the field of psychology and yourself. These pages can serve as a personal glimpse into your own mind. What you see will help you better understand the way you see yourself as well as how others see you.

This book consists of a series of paper and pencil exercises which you can complete usually alone, occasionally with a friend. Each begins with a series of instructions and includes an overview of what you are doing and why, a means to score yourself and to interpret what your score means. We have found that completing these exercise in an open and honest fashion will help you develop and expand your knowledge while showing that learning in general, and psychology in particular--can also be fun.

Nothing said to us, nothing we can learn from others,
reaches us so deep as that which we find in ourselves.
Theodore Reik

ACKNOWLEDGMENTS

Psychologically Speaking: A Self-Assessment is based upon the collected works of a large number of insightful, talented people who first wrote and developed these exercises. {Note: The preceding sentence may or may not apply to the exercises which we ourselves authored.}

All the items herein which were based upon materials written by others have [hopefully] been correctly cited as such. For readability we have on occasion rephrased or added such things as instructions for using an instrument, scoring, and/or materials on how to interpret scores. For a full and complete copy of any original items as they originally appeared, please refer to the proper citation source.

For those who have themselves been authors, they know that it is the publisher and editor who make writing a book either a pleasure to be savored or a pain to be endured. In our case working with Allyn & Bacon in general, and Sean Wakely in particular, brought out our smiles not our tears. And also, to an anonymous reviewer, (a Southern lady, social psychologist, and a feline fancier is all we know), who provided the quality of review help that most authors only dream of, who showed to us that, "Knowledge rests not upon truth alone, but upon error also" [Carl Jung], Thank You!

On a pair of personal notes:

It is only fitting and proper to take a moment to thank the many people who played a part in my own, as well as this project's development. This group includes my family (all of whose names should come equally first in this list) including Gladys, Hugh, Maxine, Edna, Cheri, and John, and to Charles and Irene to whom I owe so much; to Bruce and Lorraine Harden who adopted us when we were lost, to Dick Axen who continues to serve as my professional and intellectual "father figure"; to Robert Woodworth, the always there for me "Dutch Uncle" all graduate students hope to have but very few find; to David Madigan and especially to Cy Ulberg, instructors and mentors who became colleagues and friends; and finally to my wife Debi, and children Colin, Megan (and Josh, wherever you are) who help me enjoy my daily mortality . . .

Craig Poulenez Donovan, December 1996.

I wish to thank our students and friends who have provided the right blend of support and constructive criticism. Particular thanks are owed to Barbara, Jeff, and Kevin Rosato. Without their patience and guidance this project could not have been completed.

Peter C. Rosato, December 1996.

A REQUEST FOR HELP

We have tried hard to select and use exercises which will be both interesting and useful to one and all. However, only you, our readers and colleagues, can tell us whether and when we have succeeded in our quest. We therefore ask to you to call or write us with your comments and your suggestions.

If you see an exercise that you think would be a good one to include in our next edition, please send us a copy. In order for us to consider it, we must have a copy of the full exercise including how it is scored, etc. **and** full citation information including the magazine or other source it appeared in, the date, and page numbers. If we use your submission you will get mentioned in the next edition. In case of multiple submissions of the same item, the sender of the first copy we receive will get the acknowledgment.

Prof. Craig Poulenez Donovan
Prof. Peter C. Rosato
Kean College of New Jersey
1000 Morris Ave.
PA Department J-103
Union NJ 07083
(908) 527-3022

About the Authors:

Professor Craig Poulenez Donovan, Ph.D. is a faculty member and Director of the B.A./M.P.A. Program in the Department of Public Administration, School of Business, Government & Technology at Kean College in New Jersey. For over 15 years he has taught general and applied psychology at a variety of colleges nationwide in addition to serving as program chair. For the past 10 years he has been conducting research, teaching, and publishing in the areas of management/organizational behavior and business/governmental re-invention.

Professor Peter C. Rosato, Ph.D. obtained his doctorate degree in psychology from Hofstra University. He teaches Psychology at Kean College of New Jersey. He specializes in school psychology and learning theory.

Everything should be made as simple as possible,
but not simpler.
Albert Einstein

No law or ordinance is mightier than understanding.
Plato

Wonder is the beginning of understanding.
Greek Proverb

1

SECTION ONE: WHAT IS PSYCHOLOGY?

Psychologists are involved in many different types of activities and are confronted by different issues. Just like you, they wonder about themselves and other people. They try to see and understand how each of us is alike and how we differ in things like our personality, our intellectual abilities, our moods and our habits. They try to come up with explanations for how we got to be the way we are and why we change. The main difference between them and the average person, is that they pursue these activities on a full-time basis making a career out of the scientific study of virtually every aspect of human (and non-human) thoughts, feelings and behaviors.

The exercises which follow are intended to introduce you to the field of psychology. The first exercise explores the activities with which different types of psychologists become involved. The second one tests your knowledge of famous psychologists by using a matching format. The third and fifth exercises are about some of the difficult issues which psychologists are asked to offer opinions. One of these issues is the importance of gender roles (what is expected of males and what is expected of females). The other asks you to examine your opinion on a highly controversial topic, abortion. The other exercise in this section asks you to correctly connect a theoretical approach in psychology, with its major proponent, and finally with the belief of the approach.

It should be noted here, that not all psychologists are involved in finding out what people are like. This book and the exercises herein do examine this issue and, our focus is on the perspective of *individual differences*-the things that distinguish us from each other despite our common processes and experiences. The exercises you complete will help you gain some insights into your own thoughts and feelings. Remember however, while they are a good place to begin your inquiries into the self and your assumptions about the world, they are not a good place to end your inquires nor should they serve as absolute or conclusive data about yourself or others.

By the end of this section, you should have a better understanding of the historical figures in the field, have an appreciation of some of the topics psychologists work with, know the major schools of thought in psychology, and be adept at matching important facts and people.

What is Psychology exercises include:

1.1 Psychologists...And The Activities They Love
1.2 Famous Names & Quotes
1.3 Gender Roles
1.4 Schools Of Thought In Psychology
1.5 Your Position On...

1.1 PSYCHOLOGISTS...AND THE ACTIVITIES THEY LOVE

Many psychologists work in very different ways and in a great variety of settings. This exercise tests your knowledge of the variety within the field along with providing some insight into your own personal interests.

GOAL: To see how you are able to match up the kind of psychologist by the work they do as well as providing a gauge to your own interests.

DIRECTIONS: After reading the description of the activity, mark your level of interest in such a career with a 5 indicating high interest down to a 1 indicating no interest. After you have read and marked each activity , try to match the activity with the name of the specialty area from below.

Activity	Level of Interest	Type of Psychologist
1. Does psychotherapy and personal counselling; helps with emotional and behavioral problems; researches individual problems; and is involved in community mental health.	____	__________
2. Is involved in human relations in the workplace; tests, selects, and trains employees; performs skills analyses.	____	__________
3. Acts as a school based resource; tests school kids; evaluates classroom based programs and interventions.	____	__________
4. Tests marketing, advertising, and packaging while also studying product users and their characteristics.	____	__________
5. Detects and treats students with special learning and or school related behavioral needs.	____	__________
6. Looks at the relationship among attitudes and beliefs, personality, and disease.	____	__________

Types of psychologists are: experimental, developmental, forensic, clinical/counseling, educational, school, industrial, medical, consumer, and environmental.

Activity	Level of Interest	Type of Psychologist
7. Studies the effects of urban noise, pollution, and and crowding; serves as a consultant to architects and engineers.	____	__________
8. Works on the understanding and prevention of crimes as well as the apprehension of criminals.	____	__________
9. Seeks to understand and apply the scientific research methods to the study of the mind and behavior.	____	__________
10. Studies how people change and grow over the lifespan; works with disturbed children.	____	__________

Answers to choose from are: experimental, developmental, forensic, clinical/counseling, educational, school, industrial, medical, consumer, and environmental.

SCORING:

The correct answers are as follows:

1 - Clinical/counseling psychologist
2 - Industrial psychologist
3 - Educational psychologist
4 - Consumer psychologist
5 - School psychologist
6 - Medical psychologist
7 - Environmental psychologist
8 - Forensic psychologist
9 - Experimental psychologist
10 - Developmental psychologist

Did You Know That...

It really doesn't matter how many you got right so much as looking at the fields in which you had a high interest. The pattern of these may give you clues to the kinds of work you might like to do. For example, while three or four of the types might provide some counseling services as part of their work, only one type, the clinical/counseling psychologist regularly performs the role of therapist which most people associate with all psychologists. Experimental psychologists, for example, may do all of their work in a lab, with animals. A far cry from "listening to other people's problems."

There is only thing about which I am certain,
and that is
that there is very little about which one can be certain.
W. Somerset Maugham

1.2 FAMOUS NAMES & QUOTES

This exercise works best as a pre and post exercise. That is, at this point in your studies (the pre portion) this is mostly going to be a best guess exercise. But, taken again at the end of the course (the post portion) you should do quite well. The difference in the pre and post score is the amount of learning you have accomplished.

Famous psychologists have created and used very different terms to describe healthy, normal, well-functioning people. So, assuming you are such a person (healthy and normal that is), if you met each of these psychologists, what terms would they use to describe you?

GOAL: To see how well you know the terms used by various psychologists of different schools of psychology.

DIRECTIONS: Match the psychologists on the left with their descriptions of normality on the right by placing the letter next to the number at the bottom of this page.

Psychologist	Terms to describe normality
1. Alfred Adler	A. Self-actualized
2. Albert Bandura	B. Functioning
3. Alfred Binet	C. Fully-functioning
4. Albert Ellis	D. Individualized
5. Sigmund Freud	E. Highly developed, socially feeling
6. Carl Jung	F. Stage 5, post-conventionally moral
7. Lawrence Kohlberg	G. Formally operational
8. Abraham Maslow	H. Highly perceived self-efficacy
9. Jean Piaget	I. Rational and emotive
10. Carl Rogers	J. A spot on the intellectual bell-curve

Match the number of the psychologist to the correct letter of his description:

1. ____	4. ____	7. ____	10. ____
2. ____	5. ____	8. ____	
3. ____	6. ____	9. ____	

SCORING:

The correct answers are as follows:

1. E	6. D
2. H	7. F
3. J	8. A
4. I	9. G
5. B	10. C

If you scored 9 - 10 correctly, you either peeked at the answers or you are ready to teach this section of the course.

If you scored 7 - 8 correctly, you have a very strong knowledge base in psychology and may have career potential.

If you scored 5 - 6 correctly, you are in the range of average to above average in terms of knowledge about psychologists. This could be due to a broad exposure to the field or a variety of therapy experiences.

If you scored 4 or less correctly, don't despair, with a bit more study, you too will be scoring 10 out of 10.

1.3 GENDER ROLES

Gender roles are important to psychologists, mainly because they are a common source and example of a major force in our lives, our expectations. That is, what is "normal" is often, if unfairly, related to whether the behavior is from a male or from a female. This exercise asks for some introspection on gender roles.

GOAL: To increase your understanding of how you look at gender issues.

DIRECTIONS: In the spaces below, list ten characteristics and behaviors that you associate with being male and female in our society.

Male	**Female**
1. ________________	1. ________________
2. ________________	2. ________________
3. ________________	3. ________________
4. ________________	4. ________________
5. ________________	5. ________________
6. ________________	6. ________________
7. ________________	7. ________________
8. ________________	8. ________________
9. ________________	9. ________________
10.________________	10.________________

Part 1

Circle the numbers of ten characteristics from the twenty that you feel best apply to yourself. Did you choose any characteristics from your list of the opposite gender? If so, how many? If you found most of the characteristics you chose for yourself were from your list for your own sex, are there any characteristics from the other list you wish you did have? Do you feel our

SOURCE: This exercise, exclusive of the introduction and goal statement by Donovan and Rosato, is reprinted from *A Teacher's Tool Kit* by Bryan Strong and Christine DeVault by permission of Mayfield Publishing Company.

society's definitions of gender roles are preventing you from behaving or developing in the ways you'd most like to?

If the characteristics you chose for yourself were a mix of both lists, what do you think your description of yourself indicates about the prevailing ideas about male and female characteristics you described in our society? How valid our they?

Part 2

Recopy your list of twenty characteristics, in random order, on a new sheet of paper. Give the list to a close friend of yours who knows you well. Ask them to check each of the characteristics which they think best apply to you. When they are done, compare your list with theirs. How we see ourselves is not always how we are seen by others. How close did your matches compare with your friends? What might the differences tell you about yourself?

1.4 SCHOOLS OF THOUGHT IN PSYCHOLOGY

There are a number of different and distinct schools of thought dealing with what psychology is and what psychologists do (or should do). This exercise will test your knowledge of the different approaches, their most famous members, and how they look at people/psychology.

GOAL: To see how well you can match the various schools of psychological thought to their supporters and beliefs.

DIRECTIONS: Match the name of the approach on the left with the correct major figure for the approach and the corresponding description.

Name of the Approach	Major Figure	Schools of thought
1. Experimentalism/Structuralism	A. Freud	i. Organisms learn to respond to their environment based upon the rewards and punishments they receive.
2. Classical Conditioning	B. Rogers	ii. Behavior and feelings are based upon how individuals think they should be.
3. Operant Conditioning	C. Wundt	iii. Individuals are strongly influenced by the genetic pre-dispositions of the human species.
4. Psychodynamic	D. Pavlov	iv. The scientific method should be used to study how/why people react to the world as they do.
5. Cognitive	E. Skinner	v. Organism responses are reactions from paired external stimuli.
6. Humanistic	F. Wilson	vi. Behavior and feelings are influenced largely by unconscious thought

Name of the Approach	Major Figure	Schools of thought
7. Socio-Biological	G. Ellis	vii. Focus on personal growth and responsibility based upon core concept that all people are basically good.
8. T-Zone	H. Serling	viii. Focus on how to serve mankind (ala in a cook book).

SCORING:

The correct answers are as follows:

1 - C - iv	5 - G - ii
2 - D - v	6 - B - vii
3 - E - i	7 - F - iii
4 - A - vi	8 - H - viii

Note: Since close only counts in horseshoes, you must have *all three parts* to each answer correct to get it right.

If you scored 6 - 7 correctly, we still think you've been holding out on us and you either peeked at the answers or you are ready to teach this section of the material.

If you scored 4 - 5 correctly, you have probably learned a lot about "psychology" from TV talk shows and/or you are a cult fan of the original TV psychologist on "The Bob Newhart Show."

If you scored 1 - 3 correctly, statistics tell us this is what a reasonably good guesser would score.

If you scored 0 correctly, you may be a twisted genius since chance would say you'd get *at least* 1 right.

P.S. - If you got number 8 correct you are probably watching too much television. (Or you are a really BIG fan of the Twilight Zone and Mystery Science Theater 3000.)

1.5 YOUR POSITION ON...

Psychologists are often involved with controversial topics by helping people to clarify their attitudes about and their feelings on such topics. This exercise asks you to look at your position on just such a topic, the legality of abortions, in order to get a sense of what types of issues psychologists deal with. [Note: Controversial topics *do not* have right or wrong answers.]

GOAL: To help you define your own position on abortion

DIRECTIONS: Answer the following series of questions.

	Agree	Disagree
1. The fertilized egg is a human being from the moment of conception.	____	____
2. The rights of the fetus at any stage take precedence over any decision a woman might want to make regarding her pregnancy.	____	____
3. The rights of the fetus depend upon its gestational age: further along in the pregnancy, the fetus has more rights.	____	____
4. Each individual woman should have the final say over decisions regarding her health and body; politicians should not be allowed to decide.	____	____
5. In cases of teenagers seeking an abortion, parental consent should be required.	____	____
6. In cases of married women seeking an abortion, spousal consent should be required.	____	____
7. In cases of late abortion, tests should be done to determine the viability of the fetus.	____	____
8. The federal government should provide public funding for abortion to ensure equal access to abortion for the poor as well as the rich.	____	____
9. The federal government should not allow states to pass their own abortion laws; there should be uniform laws for the entire country.	____	____

SOURCE: This exercise, exclusive of the introduction by Donovan and Rosato, is reprinted from *A Teacher's Tool Kit* by Bryan Strong and Christine DeVault by permission of Mayfield Publishing Company.

10. Does a woman's right to choose whether or not to have an abortion depend upon the circumstances surrounding conception or the situation of the mother? In which of the following circumstances, if any, would you support a woman's right to choose an abortion (check where appropriate):

_______ An abortion is necessary to maintain the woman's life or health.

_______ The pregnancy is the result of rape or incest.

_______ A serious birth defect has been detected through amniocentesis.

_______ The pregnancy is the result of a failure of a contraceptive device.

_______ A single mother, pregnant for the fifth time, wants an abortion because she feels that she cannot support another child.

_______ A pregnant 15 year old high school student feels having a child would prove to great a disruption in her life and keep her from reaching her goals in life.

_______ A pregnant 19 year old college student does not want to interrupt her education.

_______ The father of the fetus says he will provide no support and is not interested in helping to raise a child.

_______ Parents of two boys wish to terminate the pregnancy because the fetus is male rather than female.

On the basis of your answers to the questions above, write out your position on abortion. Should it be legal or illegal? Are there certain circumstances in which it should or should not be allowed? What sorts of rules should govern when it can be performed?

2

SECTION TWO: BIOLOGY AND BEHAVIOR

Many people like to make distinctions between what is known as the "hard sciences" (biology, chemistry, physics etc.) and the "social sciences" (psychology, anthropology, figuring out what to do on a first date, etc.) This distinction, however, is sometimes easily blurred. By now, you should know that biology is the study of life and that psychology is sometimes referred to as the study of behavior. But what is life, if not behavior? The exercises in this section help you to ponder that question and others.

The first exercise is designed to show you some of the characteristics of "left-brained" and "right-brained" people. The second exercise looks at what the different sections of the brain control. The third exercise introduces you to psycho-babble by asking you to assess how you perceive your physical being. (You have to wait 'til you get there for a translation.) The next exercise asks you to look at your sleeping patterns. The final exercise attempts to determine your knowledge of drugs and their affects on the body.

Perhaps by the end of this section and these exercises you should see less of a distinction between the "hard" and the "social" sciences and appreciate why a new term has entered the field called "Biopsychology." We hope so.

Biology and Behavior exercises include:

2.1 Are You Left-Brained Or Right-Brained?
2.2 How "Brainy" Are You?
2.3 Assessing Your Body Image
2.4 Sleep Questionnaire
2.5 Drug Information Quiz

2.1 ARE YOU LEFT-BRAINED OR RIGHT-BRAINED?

Did you know that your brain has two hemispheres or sides-a right and a left? The tissue of the human brain is organized in several levels, from the more basic functions of the spinal cord and medulla to the more complex functions--thinking problem solving, perception--of the cerebral cortex, the outermost layer of the brain. The cortex is divided into the right side (on the same said as your right hand) and the left (on your left side) and these subdivisions have been found to be associated with different, complementary sets of cognitive abilities and processes. Of course, we all utilize both sides of our brains, but some of us favor one side over the other. And knowing which side you favor can help you understand a lot about yourself and become more successful at whatever you do.

To see if you have a dominant side, take this quiz by looking over sections A and B here, and check the statements that apply to you. (Be honest. Don't just mark the things you wish were true about you.)

GOAL: To see whether you are predominantly "left-brained" or "right-brained".

DIRECTIONS: Read each column and place a check next to each item which describes you.

A

___ I'm pretty good at math.
___ I keep a to-do list.
___ If I had to assemble something, I'd read the instructions first.
___ I feel comfortable expressing myself with words.
___ Before I take a stand on an issue, I like to get all the facts.
___ I always wear a watch.
___ If I forgot someone's name, I'd go through the alphabet until I remembered it.
___ I have considered becoming a lawyer, journalist or doctor.
___ I'd make a good detective.

B

___ When I talk, I gesture a lot.
___ I like to draw.
___ When I'm confused, I usually go with my gut instinct.
___ I lose track of time easily.
___ I find that sticking to my schedule is boring.
___ I am musically inclined.
___ I can tell if someone's guilty just by looking at them.
___ I've considered becoming a poet , a politician, an an architect or dancer.
___ I believe there are two sides to every story.

SOURCE: Reprinted with permission of Petersen Publishing © November 1993.

A

___ I believe there's a right and a wrong way to do everything.
___ Setting goals for myself helps me from slacking off.
___ If I have a tough decision to make, I write the pros and cons.
___ If someone asks me a question, I generally turn my head to the right.
___ If I lost something, I'd try to remember where I saw it last.
___ The expression "Life is just a bowl of cherries" makes absolutely no sense to me.

TOTAL_____

B

___ I'd rather draw someone a map than tell them how to get somewhere
___ If I have a problem, I try to work it out by relating it to a problem I've had in the past.
___ When someone asks me a question, I turn my head to the left.
___ If I don't know which way to turn, I'll let my emotions be my guide.
___ I'm always late getting places.
___ I hate following directions.
___ Some people think I'm psychic.

TOTAL_____

SCORING:

A = Left-brained
If your higher score was in the **A** column, the left side of your brain is your dominant side.

B = Right-brained
If your higher score was in the **B** column, the right side of your brain is your dominant side.

Did You Know That...

A word about cerebral hemispheres: The left hemisphere is primarily used for verbal functions such as reading, writing, and understanding language. (An easy mnemonic is that **L**eft is for **L**anguage.) The right hemisphere is more useful with nonverbal data like shapes, forms, spatial orientation, etc. An individual who has damage in the right hemisphere will likely have difficulty with a subject like geometry. A person who problems with reading or writing could have damage to the left hemisphere.

2.2 HOW "BRAINY" ARE YOU?

Our brain controls our behavior. However, the brain is not a single entity; there are many different parts to the brain and each has an impact on how we behave. What follows is an exercise designed to assess your knowledge of the relationship between a part of the brain and behavior. A warning: in real life, the parts of the brain interact and clear distinctions are not always possible.

GOAL: To investigate the relationship between areas of the brain and behavior.

DIRECTIONS: Read each sentence below and fill in the blank with the correct term from the list provided below.

1. A primary function of the ________ is to connect the cerebral hemispheres.
2. The _____ is said to house emotions.
3. Motor movement and the equilibrium are controlled by the _____.
4. Auditory stimuli are received and interpreted by the ____.
5. Forgetfulness can be blamed on a faulty _____.
6. The ____ can reasonably be called the brain's relay system.
7. Decision making and emotional control are the main functions of the ____.
8. The reception and interpretation of visual stimuli is the responsibility of the ____.
9. The ____ regulates body temperature.
10. Tactile stimuli are processed through the _____.

A. Cerebellum B. Corpus Callosum C. Frontal Lobe D. Hippocampus

E. Hypothalamus F. Limbic System G. Occipital Lobe H. Parietal Lobe

I. Temporal Lobe J. Thalamus

ANSWERS:

1.	B	2.	F	3.	A	4.	I
5.	D	6.	J	7.	C	8.	G
9.	E	10.	H.				

SCORING:

9 or 10 Correct: While not ready for brain surgery (at least not on our brains), you do have a good handle on the topic.

6 to 8 Correct: You're getting there.

5 or Fewer Correct: We told you this biology and behavior stuff was tough.

Did You Know That...

The brain can cover both extremes of function and damage. Cases have been known of children who were born with or suffered extreme brain damage early in life, who went on to have completely normal mental functioning in all ways. At the same time, brain damage after puberty usually results in permanent impairments of function. The ability of the brain to use another part of itself to take over for a damaged part is known as "plasticity." For young children the brain is quite 'plastic', a quality that is lost as we age.

2.3 ASSESSING YOUR BODY IMAGE

How we see ourselves, especially when compared to how we would like to see ourselves, is a window linking the body and the mind.

GOAL: To determine how you see/perceive your physical being (psycho-babble for your body image).

DIRECTIONS: Read each item. Circle the number which matches your feelings. You will then be asked to draw your body and your perception of an ideal body of a person of your gender. Finally, you will be asked to write about your drawings and what you think about your body.

PART 1

	Never	Sometimes	Often	Always
1. I dislike seeing myself in mirrors.	0	1	2	3
2. When I shop for clothing I am more aware of my weight problem, and consequently I find shopping for clothes somewhat unpleasant.	0	1	2	3
3. I'm ashamed to be seen in public.	0	1	2	3
4. I prefer to avoid engaging in sports or public exercise because of my appearance.	0	1	2	3
5. I feel somewhat embarrassed by my body in the presence of someone of the other sex.	0	1	2	3
6. I think my body is ugly.	0	1	2	3
7. I feel that other people must think my body is unattractive.	0	1	2	3
8. I feel that my family or friends may be embarrassed to be seen with me.	0	1	2	3

Source: *Maximize Your Body Potential* by Joyce D. Nash, Ph.D. Bull Publishing Company, Palo Alto, CA 94302, 1986. Used with permission.

9. I find myself comparing myself with other people to see if they are heavier than I am.	0	1	2	3
10. I find it difficult to enjoy activities because I am self-conscious about my physical appearance.	0	1	2	3
11. Feeling guilty about my weight problem pre-occupies most of my thinking.	0	1	2	3
12. My thoughts about my body and physical appearance are negative and self-critical.	0	1	2	3

Now, add up the number of points you have circled in each column: 0 + ____ + ____ + ____

PART 2

In the space provided, draw (1) your body and (2) your perception of an ideal body of a person of your gender.

(1) My body

(2) My idea of the ideal body

What differences do you see between your drawing of your own body and that of your ideal?

Where do your ideas about an ideal body come from?

List five positive things about your body.

1. ______________________________

2. ______________________________

3. ______________________________

4. ______________________________

5. ______________________________

Take a few moments to compare and contrast how you see yourself versus how you would like to be seen. To see how accurate your self perceptions are, ask a close friend who knows you well to complete the same questions about you and then compare their answers to your own.

PART 1 SCORING:

The lowest possible score is 0 and this indicates a positive body image. The highest possible score is 36 and this indicates an unhealthy body image. A score higher than 14 suggests a need to develop a healthier body image.

Did You Know That...

Many psychologists believe that there is a predictive relationship between a child's drawing of himself/herself and that child's body image. Those who believe that assume that drawing reflect the child's attitude toward life's stressors. Do your drawings reflect your stress?

Insomnia is a great feeder. It will nourish itself upon any kind of thinking, including thinking about not thinking.
John Ciardi

It may be that those who do most, dream most.
Stephen Leacock

2.4 SLEEP QUESTIONNAIRE

Sleep is an important biological need. However, its importance to each of us is what is known as a variable. That is, it has more importance to some of us than to others. This exercise asks you to look at the importance of sleep and other variables related to sleep.

GOAL: To evaluate your biological need for sleep.

DIRECTIONS: For each question indicate which response is most appropriate for you.

1 = Usually
2 = Often
3 = Sometimes
4 = Not Usually
5 = Never

1. I am a very light sleeper. 1 2 3 4 5
2. I wake up more tired than when I went to bed. 1 2 3 4 5
3. I fall asleep quite fast. 1 2 3 4 5
4. When I go to sleep I am physically exhausted. 1 2 3 4 5
5. I wake up at least once during the night. 1 2 3 4 5
6. As I go to sleep, I experience the physical sensation of falling. 1 2 3 4 5
7. Five or six hours of sleep are sufficient for me. 1 2 3 4 5
8. When I wake up I remember my dreams. 1 2 3 4 5
9. When I fall asleep I like to be snug and covered by blankets. 1 2 3 4 5
10. If I wake up during the night I find it difficult to fall asleep again. 1 2 3 4 5
11. Sleep is very beneficial for me. 1 2 3 4 5

SOURCE: Modified and adapted from and used with permission of George Domino, Ph.D. College of Arts and Science, Copyrighted, University of Arizona.

12. My sleep is pretty restless. 1 2 3 4 5

13. I need more than 8 hours of sleep. 1 2 3 4 5

14. My dreams are happy. 1 2 3 4 5

15. I am easily awakened by noises. 1 2 3 4 5

16. I need an alarm clock (radio or other external means) to wake up at a specific time. 1 2 3 4 5

17. When I wake up I am in a good mood. 1 2 3 4 5

18. People who know my sleep habits would probably call me a "heavy sleeper." 1 2 3 4 5

19. I wake up refreshed and rested. 1 2 3 4 5

20. I enjoy my dreams. 1 2 3 4 5

21. I fall asleep within 10 minutes of going to bed. 1 2 3 4 5

22. When I wake up I am somewhat confused and not ready to "snap to attention." 1 2 3 4 5

23. I have a favorite position in which to fall asleep. 1 2 3 4 5

24. When I remember a dream, that dream is quite vivid and detailed. 1 2 3 4 5

25. When I wake up in the morning I have worries on my mind. 1 2 3 4 5

26. I prefer to sleep with the windows open. 1 2 3 4 5

27. I look forward to sleeping late whenever I can. 1 2 3 4 5

28. I find it easy to fall asleep in a bed other than my own. 1 2 3 4 5

29. I awake from sleep because of a nightmare. 1 2 3 4 5

30. My sleep is easily disrupted when I am worried. 1 2 3 4 5

31. I have used sleeping pills to get a good night's rest. 1 2 3 4 5

32. I go to sleep most evenings at the same time. 1 2 3 4 5

33. I can sleep through a loud noise, like an alarm or the telephone ringing. 1 2 3 4 5

34. I have kept (or am keeping) a diary or my dreams. 1 2 3 4 5

35. I love to sleep. 1 2 3 4 5

36. When I have nothing to do in the evening, I go to sleep earlier than usual. 1 2 3 4 5

37. I talk in my sleep. 1 2 3 4 5

38. I can sleep with lights on in the room. 1 2 3 4 5

39. I have nightmares. 1 2 3 4 5

40. I walk in my sleep. 1 2 3 4 5

41. I can fall asleep easily in public places like an airplane, bus, or automobile. 1 2 3 4 5

42. When I wake up I am unable to move for a short time. 1 2 3 4 5

43. When I fall asleep, I literally pass out. 1 2 3 4 5

44. I prefer to sleep without any nightclothes on. 1 2 3 4 5

45. I toss and turn in my sleep. 1 2 3 4 5

46. If I am doing something interesting, I can easily stay up beyond my bedtime. 1 2 3 4 5

47. If I don't get my regular amount of sleep, I become grouchy and less efficient during the day. 1 2 3 4 5

48. My bedtime is highly irregular and varies from evening to evening. 1 2 3 4 5

49. "Early to bed and early to rise" applies to me. 1 2 3 4 5

50. My dreams are quite interesting. 1 2 3 4 5

51. I can fall asleep with the radio or television on. 1 2 3 4 5

52. I take a daytime nap. 1 2 3 4 5

53. I have physical ailments that interfere with my sleep. 1 2 3 4 5

54. I think that I may die in my sleep. 1 2 3 4 5

55. What time do you usually go to sleep in the evening? ______________________

56. What time do you usually wake up in the morning? ______________________

57. Do you take naps during the day? How many? _____ How much time (total)? _____

58. What helps you sleep better?

____

____

____

59. What interferes with your sleep?

____

____

____

Score Analysis and Interpretation:

The items have been broken into four categories (by Donovan and Rosato). Copy your scores to the chart at the end of the interpretations to examine your sleep profile.

I. SLEEP IS UNIMPORTANT OR OF POOR QUALITY. There are 17 items (1,2, 4, 5, 7, 10, 12, 15, 22, 25, 30, 31, 42, 45, 46, 48, 53) in this category. If you answered mostly 1 or 2 to these items, then one can conclude that sleep is either unimportant to you or that the quality of your sleep is poor.

II. SLEEP IS ENJOYABLE AND/OR IMPORTANT. There are 13 items (2, 3, 11, 13, 17, 18, 19, 21, 27, 35, 36, 43, 52) in this category. If you answered mostly 1 or 2 to these items, then one can conclude you enjoy sleep and/or that sleep is important to you.

III. SLEEP AND DREAMS ARE EMOTIONALLY LADEN. There are 12 items (6, 8, 14, 20, 24, 29, 34, 37, 39, 40, 50, 54) in this category. If you answered mostly 1 or 2 to these items, then one can conclude that you are a vivid dreamer and/or an active sleeper.

IV. SLEEP REGULARITY AND PHYSICAL SURROUNDINGS. There are 10 items (9, 23, 26, 28, 33, 38, 44, 47, 49) in this category. If you answered mostly 1 or 2 to these items, then one can conclude that your physical comfort and security are important to your sleeping.

Your Sleep Profile:

I	II	III	IV
1.____	3.____	6.____	9.____
2.____	11.____	8.____	23.____
4.____	13.____	14.____	26.____
5.____	16.____	20.____	28.____
7.____	17.____	24.____	32.____
10.____	18.____	29.____	33.____
12.____	19.____	34.____	38.____
15.____	21.____	37.____	44.____
22.____	27.____	39.____	47.____
25.____	35.____	40.____	49.____
30.____	36.____	50.____	
31.____	41.____	54.____	
42.____	43.____		
45.____	51.____		
46.____	52.____		
48.____			
53.____			

Note: Minor changes were made in some of the items; the scoring analysis was developed by Donovan and Rosato with reference made to the original work cited before.

A man takes a drink, the drink takes another,
and the drink takes the man.
Sinclair Lewis

Drugs are a means if you want to escape, but reality is so rich,
why escape?
Geraldine Chapman

2.5 DRUG INFORMATION QUIZ

Are You Drug Smart?

Do you see things clearly when it comes to the facts about drug use, or are you in a fog?

Take this quiz and separate the myths from the facts!

GOAL: To determine your knowledge of drugs

DIRECTIONS: Read each item and mark whether you believe the statement is a MYTH or a FACT. Then review the answers and explanations that follow.

MYTH / FACT

1. By drinking a beer or a wine cooler, a person doesn't take in as much alcohol as she would by taking a shot of hard liquor. ____
2. Taking old prescription medicine for familiar symptoms is a cost-saving and effective method of treatment. ____
3. The younger a person is when she begins drinking alcohol, the more likely she is to go on to develop alcohol dependence and alcohol-related health problems. ____
4. Athletes who take steroids are trying to increase body weight and muscular strength. Steroid use isn't the same as drug use because steroids don't affect behavior and the brain. ____
5. Marijuana isn't as damaging as other drugs because it's derived from a plant rather than chemicals. ____
6. A lot of teens try cigarettes, but few are regular smokers. ____
7. The majority of high schoolers have either used or drink alcohol on a regular basis. ____
8. Drinking a cup of caffeinated coffee can have a direct effect on a person's heart rate. ____
9. If someone drinks alcohol and doesn't feel "buzzed," it's a sign that he or she isn't consuming enough to cause any serious problems. ____

10. If a person smokes one joint, the marijuana can remain in her system for weeks. ____

11. A person who's been drinking any amount of alcohol should drink a cup of strong coffee and wait an hour before driving a vehicle. ____

12. "Crack" is a street name for tiny chunks or "rocks" of free base cocaine. ____

13. LSD use is becoming popular again because its effects only last for the duration of the "trip."____

14. Cocaine use can lead to AIDS and hepatitis. ____

15. Smoking marijuana can help some people study better because it enables them to relax and concentrate. ____

ANSWERS

1. **MYTH!** Hard liquor is often believed to be "stronger" than other alcoholic beverages; however, drinking a can or bottle of beer or a wine cooler is equivalent to drinking a shot of hard alcohol. The misuse of ANY type of alcoholic beverage can lead to alcoholism and alcohol-related health problems.

2. **MYTH!** Prescription drugs should not be viewed as permission drugs. People can develop addictions to both prescription and over-the-counter (OTC) drugs. Taking any prescription drug without medical supervision is considered a form of drug misuse.

3. **FACT!** The earlier people use alcohol, the more likely they are to abuse it, become involved with other drugs and participate in high-risk activities. Plus, alcohol is detrimental to healthy development during the teen years.

4. **MYTH!** Steroid users can subject themselves to a variety of side effects, both physical and psychological. The psychological effects can include very aggressive behavior (known as "roid rages") and depression.

5. **MYTH!** Marijuana contains over 400 chemicals, and a lot is not yet known about the damages these chemicals can do to the body. Furthermore, the average strength of marijuana has increased by 500% over the last 20 years.

6. **MYTH!** One-fifth of high-school seniors are daily cigarette smokers. Cigarettes contain some 4,000 chemicals, several of which are known carcinogens (cancer-causing agents). Perhaps

the most dangerous substance in cigarettes is nicotine, a highly addictive substance that reinforces and strengthens the desire to smoke, making it very difficult to stop.

7. **FACT!** Seven out of 10 high-school seniors have used alcohol. By age 17, half of the males who drink could be classified as "problem drinkers" because they have been drunk six times in the past year or have had trouble in school, at home or with the law because of their drinking. Rather than merely an "experimental stage," alcohol use during the high-school years can lay the groundwork for the role alcohol will play in a person's life.

8. **FACT!** Caffeine is a stimulant. It enters the bloodstream and affects the heart rate soon after being consumed. Too much caffeine can strain the heart and cause jitters throughout the body.

9. **MYTH!** Drinking alcohol but not feeling its effects can be a sign of a developing tolerance level. Tolerance means a person will need increasing amounts of alcohol to produce a "buzz" or level of intoxication. Though a person may not "feel" the effects of drinking, alcohol can still damage tissues and organs.

10. **FACT!** The chemical delta-9-THC, which produces the "high" from marijuana use, begins to build up in the fatty tissues of the body's organs after smoking just one joint. It takes at least three to four weeks for the THC from a single joint to leave the body.

11. **MYTH!** Drinking and driving DON'T mix! A person who's been drinking alcohol should never operate a vehicle. If someone is in need of a "quick fix" to make them ready for the road, it's a sure sign that the person has no business driving. Driving is a privilege allowed to SOBER people!

12. **FACT!** Crack is highly addictive form of cocaine that is absorbed directly into the bloodstream because it is smoked rather than snorted. When cocaine is inhaled directly into the lungs, it is transmitted to the brain in very concentrated amounts within eight to 10 seconds. Crack has the ability to drive its users into rapid addiction.

13. **MYTH!** LSD (lysergic acid diethylamide), the most potent of hallucinogens, can cause serious psychoactive disturbances. Nightmarish states, feelings of panic, confusion, suspicion, loss of control and flashbacks can occur long after LSD use has ceased.

14. **FACT!** In addition to its immediate effects on blood pressure, heart rate, the respiratory system and body temperature, injecting cocaine with contaminated equipment can cause AIDS, hepatitis and other diseases.

15. **MYTH!** Despite what a user might believe, marijuana use can impair and reduce her short-term memory and comprehension, alter her sense of time and reduce her ability to perform tasks requiring concentration and coordination.

You can't fake listening, it shows.
Raquel Welch

From listening comes wisdom, and from speaking repentance.
Irish Proverb

You can see a lot by observing.
Yogi Berra

3

SECTION THREE: SENSES AND PERCEPTION

In the last section, we addressed some biological issues such as cerebral hemispheric differences as correlates of behavior (see we can use big words for "Are you left-brained or right-brained?"), the need for sleep, and drug use. This section continues the biological theme but focuses on your senses and your perceptions. Psychologists do not deny the existence of reality, but observe that no one is in direct contact with reality; each of us must interpret it for ourselves. And often, our interpretations do not agree with one another. Sensation is the processing of environmental stimulation by our senses, and perception is our interpretation of what sensations mean.

Sensation deals with how we as living beings make contact with the physical world around us. We have a variety of sensing organs (our eyes, ears, nose, tongue and skin) which are stimulated by a variety of inputs (including electromagnetic waves such as visible light, acoustic waves such as sound, chemicals, temperatures and pressure).

Perception examines the complex and dynamic ways in which we interpret and organize our sensory information to create our individual and unique conscious experience of the world around us. More than just a simple decoding process, our perceptions link our senses to our memories and feelings as well as to external information about what is “out there.”

The first exercise looks at visual perception. If you have problems with it, don't worry, ask a four year old for help. The second exercise is about sensation seeking preferences. The final exercise sounded interesting to us and we hope that you find it that way also.

When this section is completed, we sense that your perception of the field of psychology will be enhanced. Put another way, our perception is that psychology will make more sense to you.

Senses and Perception exercises include:

3.1 What You Expect To See Is What You See
3.2 Identifying Your Sensation Seeking Preferences
3.3 How Are Word Sounds Discriminated?

3.1 WHAT YOU EXPECT TO SEE IS WHAT YOU SEE

This is an exercise that more four year olds will get correct than college students and it does not involve knowledge of a child's game. Intrigued? You should be. Read on.

GOAL: To determine how our expectations interfere with our perceptions.

DIRECTIONS: First, quickly count the number of aces of spades in the array of twelve cards shown on the inside cover of this book, then, flip back to this page and count the number of aces of spades on the second array of cards below.

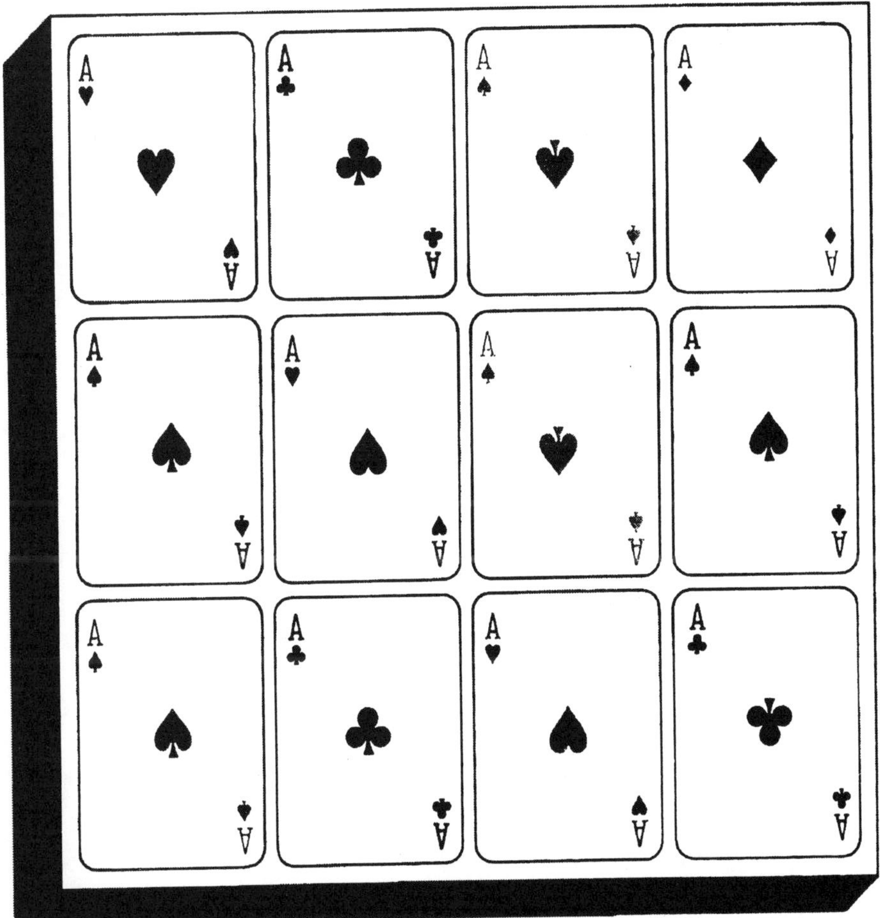

SOURCE: Adapted from and reprinted by permission from page 144 of *Adjustment and Competence: Concepts & Applications* by Grasha and Kirschenbaum;

SCORING:

Most people report that they see three. A closer examination shows that there are five. Three are black and two are of another color. Based on past experience (of which four year olds have less), we expect to the aces of spades to be black and do not look for them in a different color.

Did You Know That...

Perception is influenced by motivation. That is, what we experience is often determined by what our needs are at the time. The best example of this is the mirage of water perceived by individuals who are crossing a desert. The need for water leads people to interpret the sun's reflection on the sand as if it were a body of water. Can you think of other examples?

3.2 IDENTIFYING YOUR SENSATION SEEKING PREFERENCES

Sensation studies how individuals receive and interpret external events. Implicit in that statement is that people will respond to similar experiences in different ways. The exercise below is a fun way for you to determine what turns on your senses.

GOAL: To determine which types of activities you find pleasing to your senses.

DIRECTIONS: Answer "true" or "false" to each of the items listed below. A "true" means that the item expresses your preference most of the time. A "false" means that you do not agree that the item is generally true for you.

After completing the test, score your responses as we suggest following the test items.

T F 1. I would really enjoy sky diving.______

T F 2. I can imagine myself driving a sports car in a race and loving it.______

T F 3. My life is very secure and comfortable--the way I like it.______

T F 4. I usually like emotionally expressive or artistic people, even if they are sort of wild.______

T F 5. I like the idea of seeing many of the same warm, supportive face in my everyday life.______

T F 6. I like doing adventurous things and would have enjoyed being a pioneer in the early days of this country.______

T F 7. A good photograph should express peacefulness creatively.______

T F 8. The most important thing in living is fully experiencing all emotions.______

T F 9. I like creature comforts when I go on a trip or vacation.______

SOURCE: Reprinted by permission from page 101 of *Adjustment and Competence: Concepts & Applications* by Grasha and Kirschenbaum;

T F 10. Doing the same things each day really gets to me.______

T F 11. I love snuggling in front of a fire on a wintry day.______

T F 12. I would like to try several types of drugs as long as they didn't harm me permanently.______

T F 13. Drinking and being rowdy really appeal to me on the weekend.______

T F 14. Rational people try to avoid dangerous situations.______

T F 15. I prefer Figure "a" below to Figure ".b". ______

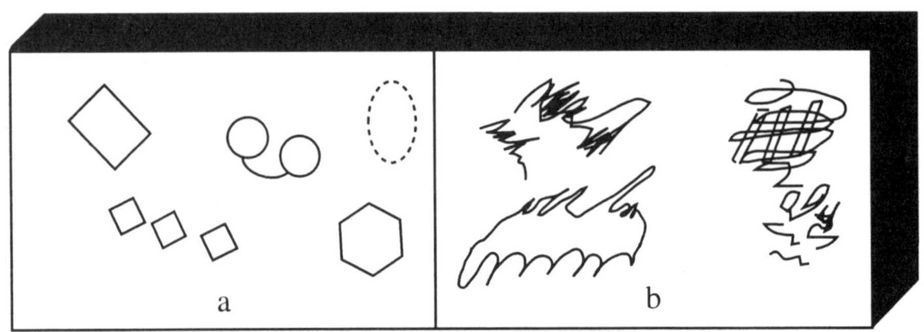

SCORING:

Give yourself 1 point for answering "true" to the following items: 1, 2, 4, 6, 8, 10, 12, and 13. Also give yourself 1 point for answering "false" to the following items: 3, 5, 7, 9, 11, 14, and 15. Get the sum of your points. Compare your total to the norms we have from people in our classes: 11-15, High sensation seeker; 6-10, Moderate sensation seeker; 1-5, Low sensation seeker.

Did You Know That...

There is a difference between sensation and perception? Sensation is the reception of stimuli by the sensors; perception is the brain's interpretation of the stimuli. Sensation occurs in sensory receptors. Perception, as we have seen, is often influenced by motivation and expectation.

3.3 HOW ARE WORD SOUNDS DISCRIMINATED?

This is an exercise which will illustrate how sound discrimination improves with age. That is, the older we get (to a point), the better we are able to perceive and make sense of sounds. Put another way, as we age our vocabulary expands and it becomes easier to match a sound with word which is stored in our memory banks. Remember, however, regional and national accents can play a major role in how and what we hear, and what others think they hear us say.

GOAL: To learn how word sound discrimination improves with age.

DIRECTIONS: Administer this test by slowly reading each word pair and asking the subject to state whether or not the words sound exactly the same. However, to make this more meaningful and more interesting (as well as more challenging), we want you to administer this to three different age groups: a child between the ages of 3 and 7; a child 8 to 15 years; and someone over the age 15.

Words in parentheses sound the same even if spelled differently.

1. think - thank
2. ears- years
3. (rat - rat)
4. grill - girl
5. chip - chick
6. false - falls
7. slow - though
8. beats- bleats
9. ass - asks
10. book - brook
11. grasp - clasp

12. patriot - patriarch

13. lamb- lamp

14. gum - gun

15. gristle - grizzle

16. then - than

17. (raze - raise)

18. (waste - waist)

19. lunch - launch

20. gram - graham

SCORING:

One would expect that a normal hearing individual over the age of 15 would get all of these items correctly; a child between the ages of 8 and 15 should only have one or two items incorrect; a younger child may have as many as four items wrong.

As a class project, you might want to graph the average number of incorrect responses by age. That is, calculate the average number of errors three year olds made and plot that on a graph. Then, do the same thing for four year olds ,etc. We predict an inverse relationship (called a negative correlation) between age and number of errors; as the child gets older, the number of errors will decrease. However, this trend will end at a certain point because errors should not be made beyond a certain age.

4

SECTION FOUR: MEMORY AND LEARNING

The exercises in this section are designed to either assess your memory or learning ability or to teach you useful techniques. The basic principles psychologists use to explain how many types of behaviors are changed by experiences are what we think of when we discuss "learning." When we talk about learning we do not mean behavioral changes that are due to such temporary conditions as being tired or sick, nor do we mean changes that come about from the natural maturation process, but only relative permanent changes. Also, you should know that psychologists have identified three basic types of learning-*classical, operant,* and *observational.*

Your ability to keep track of what you just read is a part of your cognitive system for storing and retrieving information-better known as your memory. The phenomenon of memory was one of the earliest to intrigue scientists and while much has been learned since then, understanding exactly what memory is and how it works is still one of our greatest challenges.

The first exercise in this section requires the assistance of a friend in determining your degree of forgetfulness. The next two are actual tests of memory and classification. "Storing Simple Concepts" combines learning and memory by demonstrating that item retrieval (getting information out of one's memory) is related to item storage (how information is categorized). The "Digit Span" exercise assesses your short term auditory memory (useful in remembering items such as phone numbers, zip codes etc.). The final exercise can be helpful to you by teaching you some problem solving techniques.

By the end of this section, your memory should be so good that you'll be able to...hm, we knew what we were going to say, but we forgot. Maybe we should do these exercises, if only we could remember where we put them.

Memory and Learning exercises include:

4.1 How Forgetful Are You?
4.2 Storing Simple Concepts
4.3 Digit Span
4.4 Memory And Problem Solving

4.1 HOW FORGETFUL ARE YOU?

Although we do not normally think of it in this way, our memory includes two parts, not just what we remember, but also what we forget. This exercise examines the latter, that is what you forget. To perform this exam correctly, you must be able to remember what it is you have forgotten. A second factor to keep in mind is that not all of our "forgetting" is due to our memory. Many people are able to avoid forgetting something, not because they have a good memory per se, but because they have created a good system to help them remember, such as the use of notes, etc. Having a good system is not the same as having a good memory but, remembering to use the good system is.

GOAL: To determine the extent of forgetting.

DIRECTIONS: Below are 30 common memory events. For each item, indicate how often such an event occurs to you by writing the corresponding number in the box. To get a true measure of your memory, you should conduct this twice. The first time, answer the questions about yourself. After you have done that, have a close friend answer these same questions about you.

Frequency of occurrence:

1 - Not at all in the last six months
2 - About once in the last six months
3 - More than once in the last six months but less than once a month
4 - About once a month
5 - More than once a month but less than once a week
6 - About once a week
7 - More than once a week but less than once a day
8 - About once a day
9 - More than once a day

		SELF	FRIEND
1.	Forgetting where you have put something. Losing things around your room or house.	____	____
2.	Failing to recognize places that you are told you have been to before.	____	____
3.	Finding a tv or movie story difficult to follow.	____	____

SOURCE: Adapted by Donovan and Rosato from Harris and Sutherland, MRC, Applied Psychology Unit in Cambridge.

		SELF	FRIEND
4.	Not remembering a change in your daily routine, such as a change in the place where something is kept, or a change in the time something happens. Following your old schedule or routine by mistake.	____	____
5.	Having to go back to check something to see whether you have done it or not.	____	____
6.	Forgetting when something happened.	____	____
7.	Forgetting to take something with you, or leaving things behind and having to go back and get them.	____	____
8.	Forgetting that you were told something yesterday or a few days ago and maybe having to be reminded about it.	____	____
9.	Starting to read something without realizing you have already read it before.	____	____
10.	Letting yourself ramble on to speak about unimportant or irrelevant things.	____	____
11.	Failing to recognize by sight relatives or friends whom you have known for a while.	____	____
12.	Having difficulty in picking up a new skill such as learning a new game or using a new gadget.	____	____
13.	Finding that a word is on the tip of your tongue but you just can't quite get it.	____	____
14.	Completing spacing out something you said you would do and planned to do.	____	____
15.	Forgetting something important that happened to you the day before.	____	____
16.	When talking to someone, forgetting what you just said. Maybe having to say, "What was I talking about?"	____	____

		SELF	FRIEND
17.	When reading a book or newspaper, having trouble following the thread of the story.	____	____
18.	Forgetting to tell someone something important, such as passing on a message or reminding someone of something.	____	____
19.	Forgetting important details about yourself such as your birthday or drivers license number.	____	____
20.	Getting the details of what someone has told you mixed up and confused.	____	____
21.	Telling someone a joke or story that you have already told them which they remember you telling them.	____	____
22.	Forgetting details of things you do regularly, whether at home, work, or school. For example, forgetting details of what to do, or forgetting when to do it (such as remembering to show up for class).	____	____
23.	Finding that the faces of famous people, such as seen on tv or the movies, look unfamiliar.	____	____
24.	Forgetting where things are normally kept or looking for them in the wrong place.	____	____
25.	Getting lost or turning in the wrong direction on a journey, a walk or in a building where you have OFTEN been before.	____	____
26.	Getting lost or turning in the wrong direction on a journey, a walk or in a building where you have only been once or twice before.	____	____
27.	Doing some routine things twice by mistake. For example, going to brush or comb your hair after you have just done so.	____	____
28.	Repeating to someone what you have just told them or asking them the same question twice.	____	____

		SELF	FRIEND
29.	Using the same excuse to the same professor during the same course.	____	____
30.	Forgetting the directions or the scoring key to a simple task such as this survey.	____	____

SCORING:

There are two parts to the scoring. The first is your own self-score. The second is the size of the difference between how you scored yourself and your friend's score about you. In general, a score of 27-58 means you have a good memory and are probably the person your friends ask to remind them of something they don't want to forget. A score of 58-116 is average, you won't win any prizes but you'll likely show up for your own funeral. A score of 116-243 is below average and indicates a serious problem, we just can't remember which one.

If the score you gave yourself and that given you by your friend are no more than 49 points apart, then you and your friend are doing well in gauging your forgetfulness. A difference of more than 50 points apart means you probably forget how many times you forget something, or you need a more attentive friend.

Did You Know That...

Two common explanations for forgetfulness are retroactive interference and proactive interference. If you studied Latin for two years and then studied German for two years, chances are that your knowledge of Latin will be less than if you had not taken another language. This is an example of retroactive interference. Unfortunately, in the same scenario, your memory of German will also probably be worse than if you had never taken Latin. This latter is an example of proactive interference.

4.2 STORING SIMPLE CONCEPTS

We tend to remember more easily when we can fit items into a category. The psychological term for this is concept formation. Concept formation answers the question: In which category or group does this object belong? Just like any filing system, it works only to the extent that the data can be retrieved.

GOAL: To illustrate how easy or how difficult a memory filing system works.

DIRECTIONS: Before going on to read this test, try the two sets of questions below. Be sure to time yourself on each different set.

Set 1

Name a fruit **beginning** with the letter p ________________
Name an animal **beginning** with the letter d ________________
Name a metal **beginning** with the letter I ________________
Name a bird **beginning** with the letter b ________________
Name a country **beginning** with the letter F ________________
Name a boy's name **beginning** with the letter H ________________
Name a girl's name **beginning** with the letter M ________________
Name a vegetable **beginning** with the letter p ________________
Name a weapon **beginning** with the letter s ________________

Time: ____________________________

Name a fruit **ending** with the letter h ________________
Name an animal **ending** with the letter w ________________
Name a metal **ending** with the letter r ________________
Name a bird **ending** with the letter n ________________
Name a country **ending** with the letter y ________________
Name a boy's name **ending** with the letter D ________________
Name a girl's name **ending** with the letter N ________________
Name a vegetable **ending** with the letter t ________________
Name a weapon **ending** with the letter w ________________

Time: ____________________________

SCORING:

You probably found that you were considerably quicker completing the first set than the second. On average, most people are about three times quicker. What does this imply? It tells us that the initial letter is much more important to us as an effective cue to memory than does the last letter of a word. This in turn tells us something about the way in which names are stored in our brain, since this does not necessarily need to be the case. Logically, one could design a system in which items were retrievable by the first letter, the last, second, fourth, etc. If you found that you did the last letter category as fast or faster than the first letter section, they may be a brilliant career ahead for you as a game show contestant.

Elizabeth Loftus and her colleagues have carried out a number of experiments exploring the task of coming up with a particular word, given a category and a first letter. She found that giving the category (*fruit* for example) first, and the initial letter afterwards led to faster responding than the reverse. It is as if people can activate in their minds the category of words that are a *fruit* but they cannot activate the category of all words that start with, say, *p*. This is probably because the category *fruit* is a reasonable and coherent one whereas the category of words beginning with *p* would be far too large to be useful.

The same phenomenon came from a study in which the category used was *type of psychologist*, and the initial letter was that of the first letter of the person's name. Hence a typical question might be "Give me a developmental psychologist whose name begins with a *P*" (Piaget) versus, "Initial letter *P*, a developmental psychologist." Students who were just beginning to study psychology showed no difference between the two orders of presentation, but those who had already specialized were faster when the category came first. Presumably, they had already developed categories such as "developmental psychologists" and were able to use them while new students had to search all psychologists and then try to recategorize them afterwards.

4.3 DIGIT SPAN

The question of the capacity of immediate memory was one which preoccupied a number of philosophers during the 19th century. Sir William Hamilton, for example, observed that if one flung a handful of marbles on the ground, the maximum number that could be perceived reasonably accurately would be about seven. The first systematic experimental work to be done on this subject was carried out in 1887 by a London schoolteacher, J. Jacobs, who was interested in measuring the mental capacity of his pupils. He devised a technique, the digit span, which has played an important role in psychology ever since. It is used in many psychological exams even to this day.

The procedure is as follows. The subject is presented with a sequence of numbers (or digits) and is required to repeat them all back in exactly the same order that he/she heard them. The length of the sequence presented is steadily increased until a point is reached at which the subject always fails to be able to repeat all the digits in the correct order.

GOAL: To determine your short term auditory memory of digits.

DIRECTIONS: Have someone read you each of the following rows of numbers on the next page, one at a time (don't peek!). They should be read at a steady rate (at about 2 numbers per second). As soon as the numbers in a row are read, you must close your eyes and repeat them all back out loud, in exactly the same order. Your friend should place a check mark next to each row as your repeat it successfully. Do the first row, then the second and so on until you fail to get two rows correct.

Row A	9 7 5 4
Row B	3 8 2 5
Row C	6 5 1 4
Row D	9 4 3 1 8
Row E	6 8 2 5 9
Row F	3 8 1 4 7
Row G	9 1 3 8 2 5
Row H	6 4 8 3 7 1
Row I	5 9 6 3 8 2
Row J	7 9 5 8 4 2 3
Row K	5 3 1 6 8 4 2
Row L	7 9 1 8 5 4 6
Row M	8 6 9 5 1 3 7 2
Row N	5 1 7 3 9 8 2 6
Row O	5 1 3 9 8 2 4 7
Row P	7 1 9 3 8 4 2 6 1
Row Q	1 6 3 8 7 4 9 5 2
Row R	6 1 5 9 4 3 8 2 6
Row S	9 1 5 2 4 3 8 1 6 2
Row T	7 1 5 4 8 5 6 1 9 3
Row U	1 5 2 8 4 6 7 3 1 8

SCORING:

Count the number of digits present in the last row you got correct. While most people can manage six or seven digits, there is a large range of variation, with some people managing only four or five while other five while others can get up to ten or more.

Did You Know That...

Memory for digits, for most of us, peaks at about age thirteen. This means, that under normal circumstances, the memory for digits of an eighth grader is about the same as that of an equally intelligent college student. Individuals who have difficulty with this task are sometimes viewed as overly anxious. Their anxiety interferes with their ability to concentrate on the stimuli.

For a variation on the exercise presented, you might want to try "digits backwards." Have someone read you the digits slowly. When the set is read, you are to repeat them backwards. For example, 9-7-5-4 would become 4-5-7-9. Obviously, this is a much more challenging task.

4.4 MEMORY AND PROBLEM SOLVING

There is a strong relationship between remembering and problem solving. We believe that people who are good at remembering information have developed effective problem-solving skills. First, they are able to *identify* and *define* situations that may cause memory difficulties ("this is too much information to hold in short-term memory" or "if I am not careful I will get confused and forget whether 'port' means right or left"). Second, they *explore* a variety of strategies and realize the need to select those appropriate for a particular memory task. Third, they *actively* try strategies and *look* at the effects on performance (that is, on their ability to remember). If their performance is poor, they rethink their strategies and perhaps redefine the nature of the problem or select or invent different strategies. They then act on these changes and look at the effects, and hence continue to improve their memory skills.

The improvement of memory skills is an ongoing process. A major challenge is to become skilled at inventing new memory techniques for solving problems you may confront in everyday life. The following will allow you to test and strengthen your memory abilities.

GOAL: To illustrate methods of improving memory and problem solving skills.

DIRECTIONS: Carefully read the passage below once, and then check the answer section and answer the questions about it.

1. You are the driver of a bus that can hold a total of 72 passengers (there are 36 seats that can each hold 2 passengers). At the first stop 7 people get on the bus. At the next stop 3 people get off and 5 get on. At the next stop 4 people get off and 2 get on. During each of the next two stops, 3 passengers get off and 2 get on. At the next stop 5 passengers get off and 7 get on the bus. When the bus arrives at the next to the last stop, 2 people get on and 5 get off.

Develop acronyms or other techniques for remembering the following.

2. The order of the cranial nerves is olfactory, optic, oculomotor, trochlear, trigeminal, abducens, facial, auditory, glossopharyngeal, vagus, spinal-accessory, and hypoglossal.

3. You should set the clock 1 hour ahead in the spring and an hour back in the fall (for daylight savings time).

Devise strategies for remembering the following.

4. The combination to your new lock is 22-4-9.

5. Balsam fir trees have smooth twigs; Eastern hemlocks have rough twigs.

Devise a strategy to help you remember the correct spelling for each word below.

	Correct spelling	*Common misspelling*
6.	across	accross
7.	facilitate	facillitate
8.	development	developement

Devise a technique for remembering the facts associated with each name when you are presented with the name.

9.	Edmund Hillary:	First to climb Mount Everest
10.	Hubert Booth:	Invented the vacuum cleaner
11.	Frank T. Cary:	Former chairman of IBM

ANSWERS

1. How many stops did the bus make?

   Most people are not prepared for this question. They anticipated a different question; namely, “How many people were left on the bus?” Different strategies are necessary to prepare for these different questions. This is a good illustration of how various strategies may or may not be most appropriate depending on the memory problem one is attempting to solve.

   What is the name of the bus driver?

   Most people have a difficult time answering this question from memory because they cannot remember being told about anyone's name. If you look back at the first sentence of the passage, you will see that the answer to this question is quite familiar to you.

2. An acrostic for remembering the cranial nerves that has been around for some time is: "On old Olympus' towering tops a Finn and German vend some hops."

3. A helpful acrostic for remembering whether to set one's clock forward or back an hour is, "Spring forward and fall back."

4. You could combine the rhyme peg word system (one is a bun, two is a shoe, and so on) and an acrostic in the following manner. Think of the acrostic, "You must wear two shoes to get in the door and stand in line,".... From the peg word system you know that "two is a shoe," so two shoes equals 22. Similarly, you know from the peg word system that "four is a door" (so, door helps you remember the number 4) and that "nine is a line" (so, line helps you remember the number 9).

5. You could use acrostics, such as "fir is smooth" and "a rough hem stands out." For the latter, think of "hem" as short for hemlock and think of "standing out" as illustrating a rough twig.

6. For "across," an example using acrostics is, "You only cross the gate to heaven once." Let "across" remind you of "cross" and let "once" remind you of the number of *c*'s.

7. For "facilitate," you might state to yourself that, "The face of a penny has one picture of Lincoln." Let facilitate remind you of "face" and let the thought of one picture of Lincoln (which begins with an *l*) remind you that there is only one *l*.

8. For "development," you might think, "When you want to develop film, people should not enter the darkroom while the process is going on." Let "development" remind you of develop (as in develop the film) and let "do not enter" remind you of "no e" after develop.

9. You might imagine someone climbing a big hill (for the first part of his last name) and use the sound of last part of his name (Hillary--e) to signify Everest.

10. One possibility is to let the "bert" part of Hubert remind you of dirt and the "Booth" remind you of boots. Dirt left by boots needs to be removed, preferably by a vacuum cleaner.

11. You could let the "rank" in Frank remind you of rank, let the middle initial (*t*) remind you of "tops," and let the *c* in Cary remind you of computers. Thinking about "ranks tops in computer sales" could then help you remember his position in IBM (assuming that you are familiar with the fact that IBM is a leader in sales of computers).

5

SECTION FIVE: THINKING AND LANGUAGE

All of the exercises in this section are designed as learning and thinking aids. That is, rather than just assess what you know about thinking and language, we thought that it would be more helpful to give you some extra tools which you can employ in a variety of classes and in other daily situations. Another way to say that is that these exercises can be viewed as mental gymnastics. Can mental exercises really boost thought power the way physical exercises improve physical fitness? You bet! Read on and begin reaping the benefits!

Our first task looks at creative methods to solve everyday problems. Some of the items make use of the left side of your brain, some of the right side, and some require shifts from one side to the other. (That is why we needed for you to know if you were left- brained or right-brained in section two.)

The second exercise could be placed in a couple of different sections. It deals with how to relax. One of the greatest aids to solid, creative thinking is to be relaxed. It is also very good for you in terms of your overall stress and health.

The third set of problems looks at your ability to think logically. As you may know, psychology is a branch of philosophy which studies logical thought patterns. Even if you get these items incorrect, take the time to discover the reason for the correct answer.

The final exercise continues this logic theme. It requires you to look at problems and to generate possible solutions.

Although you will not be ready to argue cases before the Supreme Court, or even be able to convince a professor to change your grade, by the end of this section you should be able to think more logically and to be able to express yourself more exactly. And who knows, maybe you'll win an argument with yourself.

Thinking and Language exercises include:

5.1 From Criticism to Creativity
5.2 Relaxation is Just a State of Mind
5.3 How Well Can You Explain It All
5.4 Logic and Erroneous Thinking

5.1 FROM CRITICISM TO CREATIVITY

The approach to problem solving developed by Bransford and Stein can enhance creativity. Unlike many popular accounts of creativity, which seem to suggest that novel ideas simply "come from nowhere," the importance of identifying and defining the basic assumptions that underlie their approach to particular problems ("I'm too old to retrain for a new job," or, "These experts know everything I know plus more") are keys to success. These assumptions often keep us from approaching problems in more creative ways.

It would be nice if we could simply ask ourselves about the basic assumptions we are making and have this information immediately available to us. Unfortunately, we generally cannot do this; many of our assumptions are implicit and hence are not directly available to the consciousness. Nevertheless, there are strategies such as looking for inconsistencies, making predictions, analyzing the worst case, and seeking criticism from others. These strategies do not guarantee we will uncover all our implicit assumptions, but they certainly help.

Also important are the recognition of assumptions ("We have been considering only conventional uses for our bricks") provides no guarantee one will be able to generate a wide range of possible alternatives. There are a number of strategies that can increase the generation of novel ideas. These include the analysis of problems into components, the use of analogies, brainstorming, incubation, and active attempts to communicate. When used appropriately, these strategies can help us approach problems in much more creative ways.

Let's see how creative you can be. Try each of the exercises below.

EXERCISES

1. Generate some inventions (ones that you make up as well as ones that you already know about) that can help people appreciate the sights and sounds of tropical fish while remaining in their homes (one invention would be an aquarium). Generate as many as you can within 3 minutes.

2. Two men played checkers. They played five games, and each man won three. How is this possible?

3. Six normal drinking glasses are standing in a row. The first three are full of water; the next three are empty. By handling and moving only one glass, change the arrangement so that no full glass is next to another full glass, and no empty glass is next to another empty one.

4. Generate as many reasons as you can why, when my cousin comes to visit me in my apartment, he always gets off the elevator five floors below my floor and walks the rest of the way.

5. How could you make a tennis ball go a short distance, come to dead stop, then reverse itself and go in the opposite direction? *Note*: Bouncing the ball is not permitted, nor can you put spin on the ball and roll it (this is really a form of bouncing it) or tie anything to the ball.

6. Look at the nine dots drawn below. The problem is to connect all of them by using only four straight lines and never retracing a line or removing your pen or pencil from the table as you draw.

. . .

. . .

. . .

7. Draw the roman numbers for nine (the capital letters IX). Now, add one line to your IX to make six.

8. Try solving this mystery.

A county sheriff arrived at the scene of an apparent homicide and found the victim lying on the side of the road, dead. The only clue to the crime was a pair of tire tracks left on the little-traveled dirt road. The sheriff followed the tracks to a country farmhouse less than a mile away. Although there were three men sitting on the front porch, the sheriff was certain that the man he wanted for questioning was sitting in the middle even though he knew that none of the men had a car and none had mud on their boots. How did the sheriff know he should question the man sitting in the middle?

9. Do you see any inconsistencies in the passage below? If so, are there ways they might be resolved?

The man was worried. His car came to a halt, and he was all alone. It was extremely dark and cold. The man took off his overcoat, rolled down the window, and got out of the car as quickly as possible. Then he used all his strength to move as fast as he could. He was relieved when he finally saw the lights of the city, even though they were far away.

SCORING-ANSWERS:

1. Most people generate such items as a magnifying glass, an underwater sound amplifier, or an underwater light. These are all fine answers, but it is nevertheless useful to ask whether they are constrained by various implicit assumptions.

   Most people generate inventions designed to help people enjoy actual fish that live in an aquarium; therefore they make an implicit assumption that is unnecessary. The problem of helping people enjoy the sights and sounds of tropical fish in their own homes could also be solved by inventing an aquarium videotape. In fact, such tapes are on the market and can be bought in many video stores.

2. The men did not play one another. The assumption that they *did* play one another renders the problem insolvable.

3. The simplest solution is to pick up the second glass from the left and pour the water from it into the next to last glass on the right. Many people fail to generate this solution because they make the implicit assumption that the water cannot be poured from one glass into another.

4. Most people generate such reasons as

   --Wants to exercise.
   --Needs to exercise.
   --Wants to surprise you.
   --Wants to visit someone on the way.
   --The elevator is broken.

   These all involve assumptions that the cousin is essentially normal. An alternate possibility is that the cousin is so short he cannot reach the higher buttons. He therefore punches the highest button he can reach and walks from there.

5. The most obvious solution to this problem is the one least frequently generated. Simply throw the ball straight up in the air. It will stop and eventually reverse its direction.

6. The most common error on this problem is to make the assumption that you must stay within the imaginary lines that form the square. The solution illustrated below goes outside these imaginary lines.

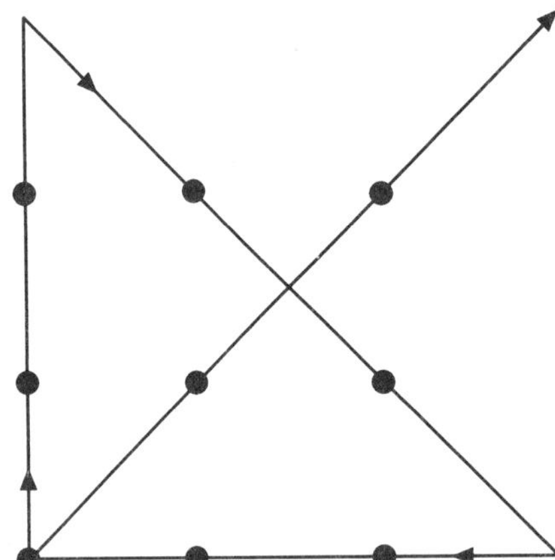

7. The most common error with this problem is to assume one is dealing with Roman numerals. If you think of the numbers as Arabic numerals, the answer is simply: six.

8. This problem is similar to the classic nine-dot problem in that people tend to make assumptions that are not necessarily true and that make a solution impossible. In this case most people make the assumption that the tire tracks were produced by a car. The only reason the sheriff knew which man he wanted was because the tire tracks were produced by a wheelchair and man sitting in the middle of the porch was in a wheelchair.

9. A seeming inconsistency in the passage is that the man took off his overcoat, yet the passage said it was cold and dark. At first glance this appears to be an illogical thing to do. Imagine the we make the assumption that the car had fallen into a lake ("his submerged car came to a halt..."). Now, the apparent inconsistency between the cold temperature and the act of removing the coat is resolved.

5.2 RELAXATION IS JUST A STATE OF MIND

This is an exercise designed to teach you how relax. The techniques which follow should be helpful to you whenever stress approaches (term paper time; exams are impending; your favorite team is about to lose a big game).

GOAL: To teach you methods of relaxing.

DIRECTIONS: Sit back (or lie down), relax, have someone read each item to you; do as you are asked. (You might also want to tape this for yourself.) Do this in a quiet environment. To help you relax, think of the most pleasant setting you can perhaps lying on a raft in a swimming pool, or sitting in a lounge chair with your feet elevated.

(Start by taking a deep breathe - through your nose - hold it for 10 seconds - exhale through your mouth.)

1. Relax and allow your muscles to go limp.

2. Start with the top of your head; sense the muscles in your head and allow them to relax. Release any tension.

3. Now have the relaxation move to your forehead; allow any tension to dissipate.

4. The muscles over your eyelids are next; have them relaxed.

5. Move to your facial muscles; relax them.

   Take another deep breathe as above. Hold for 10 seconds; exhale through your mouth.

6. Relax your neck muscles.

   (Think of a pleasant site on a beach if you have any trouble relaxing.)

7. Relax your shoulder muscles; let them fall limp. Imagine that they are very heavy and that you cannot hold them up any longer.

8. Do the same with your arms - start with your heavy right arm and then your left arm.

9. Release the tension in your trunk muscles.

Time for another deep breathe. Breathe deeply but **slowly**. Hold ....exhale.

10. Now relax your right leg and foot. Think of how heavy they are. Let them fall limp.

11. Finally, do that with left leg and foot.

Take a deep breathe again.

Note: This exercise utilizes techniques developed by the following: H. Benson, (1975). *The relaxation response*. New York: Morrow Press; and E. Jacobson, (1974). *Progressive relaxation*. Chicago: University of Chicago Press.

5.3 HOW WELL CAN YOU EXPLAIN IT ALL?

Our ability to understand and explain the reasons for why things happen are a central part of our thinking skills. The three questions below are part of series of such questions used to analyze critical thinking skills.

See how well you can reason out the correct response to each.

GOAL: To illustrate examples of logical thinking.

DIRECTIONS: Read Fact 1 and Fact 2 below, then answer the question underneath the facts.

1. Fact 1 - A camper started a fire to cook food on a windy day in a forest.
   Fact 2 - A fire started in dry grass near a campfire in the forest.

   Both of these facts took place in the same forest. Could one have at least partly caused the other?

   a. Yes; Fact 1 could have at least partly caused fact 2.
   b. Yes; Fact 2 could have at least partly caused fact 1.
   c. No; neither is likely to have caused the other.

2. Fact 1 - A camper started a fire to cook food on a windy day in a forest.
   Fact 2 - A fire started in dry grass near a campfire in the forest.

   Could any of the following statements be used to explain any of the possible cause-and-effect connections between Facts 1 and 2? If so, which *one* would be best?

   a. The heat from burning trees can set other trees on fire.
   b. Burning coals from a campfire are hot enough to start a fire in dry grass.
   c. Food requires heat for cooking.
   d. None of these.

3. Fact 1 - A camper started a fire to cook food on a windy day in a forest.
   Fact 2 - A fire started in dry grass near a campfire in the forest.

SOURCE: Wallen, N. E., Durkin, M. C., Fraenkel, J. R., McNaughton, A. H. and Sawin, E. I. *The Taba Curriculum Development Project in Social Studies.* Final report, Project No. 5-1314, Grant No. OE-6-10-182, U.S. Department of Health, Education and Welfare. San Francisco State College, California, 1969. ERIC document no. ED 040106.

Here is another fact that happened later that day in the same forest:

Fact Y - A house in the forest burned down.

Imagine that you have been asked to explain what might have caused the house to burn down in Fact Y. Could facts 2 and 1 be useful as part of the explanation?

a. Yes; both 1 and 2 and the cause-and-effects between them would be useful.
b. Yes; both 1 and 2 would be useful even though neither was likely a cause of the other.
c. No; because *only one* of Facts 1 and 2 was a likely cause of Y.
d. No; because *neither* 1 or 2 was a likely cause.

Did You Know That...

Psychologist Jean Piaget first put forth the concept of developmental stages for thinking skills. To solve the problems in this exercise, an individual must have had to reach, at a minimum, the Stage of Formal Operations. Individuals of normal intelligence generally reach this stage in early adolescence. During the Stage of Formal Operations, the individual is able to conceptualize hypothetical situations and to engage in scientific thinking.

The Correct Answers are as follows:

1. a
2. b
3. a

5.4 LOGIC AND ERRONEOUS THINKING

There are three general ways in which arguments may be faulty. One is that they may be based on inaccurate factual claims ("These data prove that more exposure to computers increases peoples liking for them"). Note that people who make such claims are not necessarily trying to be misleading or dishonest. Instead, they frequently fail to realize their interpretations are in error.

A second reason arguments may be faulty involves the use of inappropriate logic. People may begin with an acceptable factual claim ("Many people who eventually fall in love started out not liking each other") yet end with a conclusion that does not follow from the facts ("Therefore, this person who dislikes me now, will eventually fall in love with me"). Similarly, people may make arguments that contain inconsistencies. When writing a paper, for example, an author may at first state that an historical figure never changed his mind about a particular issue yet later provide an example indicating that he did indeed change his mind.

A third reason for criticism involves the assumptions that form the basis of the argument. People's arguments will frequently seem valid if we grant them their initial assumptions ("Since war is inevitable, we should make the first strike"). However, once the basic assumptions are identified and questioned ("What makes you think that war is inevitable?"), arguments frequently lose their initial force. We also emphasized that the use of analogies and metaphors involves assumptions that may or may not be appropriate. Unless these are analyzed explicitly, they can lead us astray.

GOAL: To develop your ability to apply intelligent criticism.

DIRECTIONS: Read each statement. On a sperate sheet of paper answer each of the questions below to the best of your ability.

1. What do you conclude from the statement, "Nine out of ten doctors surveyed recommended this product?"

2. What additional information would you want to know in order to evaluate the claim, "American school children scored lower on mathematics achievement tests than did children in all other industrialized countries." (Assume that all children were of comparable ages and all received comparable achievement tests.)

3. What are some possible problems with the following factual claim? "Our teachers are better than those at University X. Students who have graduated from our University averaged $10,000 more per year than did students who graduated from University X."

4. A school survey reveals that students who have computers at home earn significantly better grades than students who do not have computers at home. Should the school recommend that parents buy their children computers?

5. In 1927, Elton Mayo began a study at his plant to investigate the effects of illumination intensity on worker productivity. One of the findings in that investigation revealed that, when the illumination level was increased at the plant, productivity went up. If you were the plant manager, would you increase the lighting provided for workers at the plant? Why or why not?

6. If all men in Scottberg live on Gorky Street and no people who live on Gorky Street love strawberry pie, can we logically conclude that some men who live in Scottberg love strawberry pie?

7. If all xenos are oxons and some oxons are red, can one conclude that all xenos are red?

8. If all xenos are oxons and all zeeps are xenos , can one conclude that all zeeps are oxons.

9. Assume that the following is true: "If I go to the party I cannot do my homework." If I did not do my homework, can one conclude I went to the party?

10. To test a theory that RNA is used to store information in the brain, scientists injected 20 people with RNA. They found that the 20 people performed no better on a memory test after they were injected with RNA than before they were injected with RNA. Have they disproved the theory that RNA is used to store information in the brain?

11. Read the following game rules and then answer the questions below.

    This is a two-player game. Each player starts at opposite corners of a checkerboard. The players move around the outside edge only. The object of the game is to reach the other player's corner first. This player rolls the dice, and the player with the highest roll goes first. This player also picks a direction, either clockwise or counterclockwise. The other player must move in the opposite direction. On each turn the dice are rolled and the player with the highest roll advances one square on the board. The other player does not move on that turn. Players cannot occupy the same square at the same time.

    A. Does the player who moves first have an advantage?

    B. How long would the average game last?

    C. If you played 100 games, how many would you expect to win?

12. You are at a crossroads and need directions about which path to take to the nearest town, but you don't know if the only person there to help you is a liar or truthful. If he is truthful he will always answer truthfully; if he is a liar, he will always answer untruthfully. Using only one question, how can you find out which path is correct?

13. There are two brothers, one of whom always tells the truth and other always lies. The truthful brother is very knowledgeable and always answers correctly; the liar is very poorly informed and always thinks things are just the opposite of how they really are. Since the liar is both poorly informed and lies, he will usually answer questions identically to his brother. For example, the liar would answer yes to the question, "Is two plus two equal to four?" because he thinks that 2 + 2 is not equal to 4, but lies about it. Can you ask one question requiring a yes or no answer that will tell you which brother you are talking to?

ANSWERS

Score yourself on a scale from 1-10 for each questions based on how well your answer/thinking matches the answers below.

1. This statement encourages the reader to make many inferences, but what it actually means could be quite different from those invited inferences. For example, it could mean that nine of ten doctors surveyed have at one time or another recommended this product to at least one person (not necessarily a patient and not necessarily to the exclusion of other similar products). It does not necessarily mean that the doctors prefer this product or advise patients to use it more than any other product. Try to think of some unusual products or substances that could legitimately fit this claim.

2. Assuming that all the children were of a comparable age and received comparable achievement tests, we would still want to have additional information, especially about the samples of students who were tested. Was the average score for American children lowest simply because all American children are encouraged to go to school, even those who are not interested, whereas other countries may not include such children in the sample who took the test? Some data relevant to this question would be whether the best American students (the top one-third) did as well as the best in other countries. This would say something about whether the average scores say more about sampling than about the quality of instruction students receive.

3. There are a number of possible problems with this statement. One reason for higher incomes is that the first school may teach courses (like business) that usually result in higher salaries than those taught by the second school (like education).

   A second reason may be that the first university may have been in operation much longer; hence, its graduates have had time to earn higher salaries because of their seniority.

A third reason is that the first university may attract better students in the first place. They may graduate and earn more only because they began at a higher level, not because the instructional program is inherently better.

4. The relationship between grades and computers is correlational. Computers at home could contribute to better grades, but it is also possible that students who get better grades are more likely to take an interest in computers or that parents who take an active role in stimulating their child's intellectual development influence their children to perform better in school and are more likely to buy home computers to improve the learning environment at home. If the school board wanted to know if computers at home actually influenced performance at school, they would need to conduct a controlled experiment.

5. The finding is part of a series of investigations known as the Hawthorne studies, which were conducted at the Western Electric Hawthorne plant. The findings are indicative of what some have labeled the Hawthorne effect. In these investigations worker productivity seemed to improve regardless of the illumination level under which workers operated. For example, in one experiment the lighting was reduced to the intensity of ordinary moonlight and subjects still maintained their production level. In another study, when light bulbs were replaced with bulbs of the same intensity, subjects reported that they liked the increased illumination. These results are often used to illustrate the effects management can have on worker productivity when workers think management is taking an increased interest in their problems.

6. No. None of the men who love strawberry pie live on Gorky Street. See the diagram below.

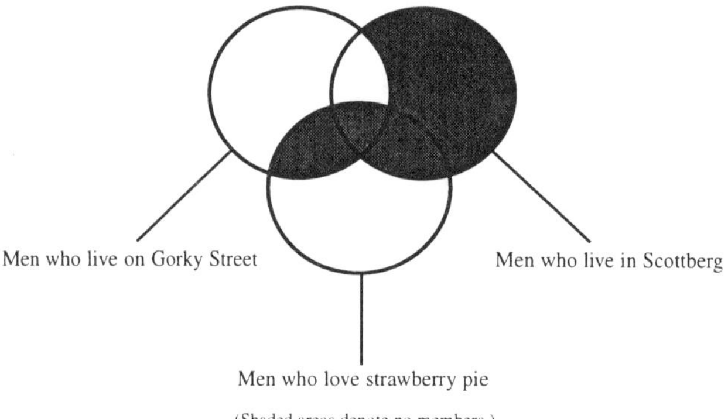

7. No. It is possible that some xenos are not red. See the diagram below.

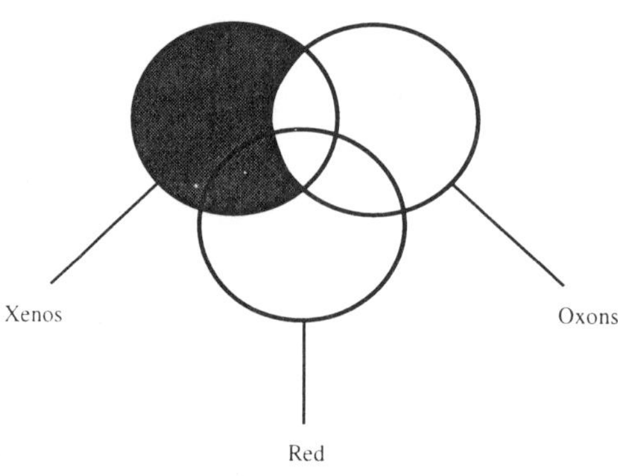

8. Yes. See the diagram below.

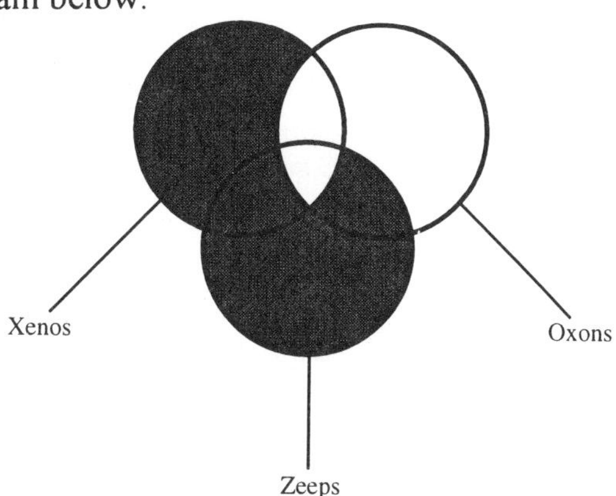

(Shaded areas denote no members.)

9. No. I may have skipped the party yet stilled failed to do my homework. The form of reasoning being used here is: If A (go to party), then B (cannot do my homework). If one were to reason "B, therefore A," one would committing the fallacy of affirming the consequent.

10. Although the form of logical reasoning that leads to such a conclusion is valid, this is a clear case in which one is testing not only a theory but also additional assumptions that relate that theory to observable data. For example, it is possible that the theory is correct and yet injections of RNA will have no immediate effect on memory. It is also possible that the site of the injection could be an important determinant of the effect observed, that the injection must be given several days in advance, and so forth.

11. This game will have no winner because players will quickly encounter a situation in which neither player can advance without breaking the rule of never occupying the same square simultaneously.

12. The first step is to define the problem. What information is being requested: Is the problem to differentiate the liar from the one who is truthful or simply to obtain correct directions? In the first problem the task is to obtain correct directions. Since only one question can be asked, the problem really becomes, "What question will the liar and one who is truthful both answer correctly?" Lying is negating the truth, so one might think about situations in which negation or negatives can be eliminated. For example, in grammar a double negative is really a positive number. To use a similar strategy in this problem, we would need to ask a question that required the liar to lie twice. One way to do this is to ask a question that requires the person to answer how they would answer, for example, "If I asked you if this was the correct path would you say yes?"

13. In the second problem the task is really to differentiate the liar from the brother who tells the truth or to formulate a question that each will answer differently. This problem is related to the previous example in that it involves a double negative--the liar lies but is

always misinformed--so the answer is correct. When will the two brothers answer questions differently? Since both the truthful brother and the liar will give an answer that is usually correct, all we need to do is to ask either of them about themselves or the other brother. For example, if asked, "Are you a liar?", the truthful brother would say no. The liar would think he wasn't a liar but would lie about it and say "yes." A question such as, "Is your brother a liar?" will produce similar results.

6

SECTION SIX: INTELLIGENCE AND MEMORY

To many people, one of the most important dimensions in our analyses of ourselves and others has to do with our ability to think abstractly and to learn readily from experience-the dimension that we call intelligence. There are many ways to measure intelligence; there are also many aspects of intelligence. The items in this section look at only one type of intelligence, verbal intelligence. (This may also be called crystallized intelligence because it is said to be formed or learned.) We selected this type of intelligence because it has the highest correlation (relationship to) with success in school.

Our goal is to show you some samples of the types of items typically found on current and past tests of intelligence. Bear in mind that intelligence tests are tried out on large numbers of people who fit certain demographic characteristics. The results are then tabulated and norms are developed. From there, raw scores are converted to standard scores and IQs result. We make no pretense about attempting to measure your IQ. There are enough bogus methods out on the market that inaccurately do that.

The first exercise is what is commonly called an "unusual uses" test. It tests a form a verbal intelligence which is closely related to verbal creativity. People successful on these items are probably good at writing and tasks such as crossword puzzles.

Another measure of verbal skills is the "Intelligent Understanding of Proverbs". This task looks at your ability to decipher expressions. There is an element of social intelligence here as you are asked to determine what is commonly meant by the proverb. The exercise we call "Word Pairs" is used on tests today. The idea was also used in the past. The items measure your ability to see the relationship between two words.

The final exercise comes from the predecessor of some of today's tests. It is a problem solving task involving language and mathematics. We hope that you'll have fun with it.

Intelligence and Creativity exercises include:

6.1 You Want Me To Do **What** With A...?
6.2 Intelligent Understanding Of Proverbs
6.3 Word Pairs
6.4 Water, Water Everywhere

6.1 YOU WANT ME TO DO *WHAT* WITH A ...?

There is often a fine line between intelligence and creativity. Creative individuals need a certain degree of intelligence or their "creations" would be eccentricities. However, a person can be intelligent without being creative.

The following exercise allows you to test your creativity while using your intelligence. You will be asked to write unusual uses for common items. For example, can you name three *unusual* uses for a brick? Well, a brick can be a weapon, a paperweight, or a tool (like a hammer).

GOAL: To demonstrate one form of verbal creativity.

DIRECTIONS: Try to think of at least three *unusual* uses for each item listed below. Verify your answers with a partner. To receive credit for your response, your partner must be able to explain how the item could be used in the way that you mention. Your partner must also agree that the use mentioned is indeed *unusual*.

Name three *unusual* uses for :

1. A pencil
2. A mattress
3. A tire
4. Marbles
5. An empty bottle
6. A hard cover book
7. A garden hose section
8. A paper clip
9. A table spoon
10. A hair brush

POSSIBLE ANSWERS:

1. A pencil: for poking holes; a substitute cotton swab (Q Tip); a pacifier (how many of you chew on pencils?); a drum stick.

2. A mattress: a door blocker; a trampoline; a soft landing space to escape from a fire; a bank vault.

3. A tire: a swing; an exercise site (football players run through tires); a target for throwing balls through; a bumper guard.

4. Marbles: to trip people (remember Home Alone); tangible counters (to aid in arithmetic); decorations; hand exercise.

5. An empty bottle: vase; portable toilet; candlestick holder; musical instrument.

6. A hard cover book: door stop; seat elevator (small children can sit on books to better reach the table); hider of a wall safe; posture perfecter (put book on your head).

7. A garden hose section: imitation snake; garrote (to strangle someone); fire escape rope; a border to separate a lawn from shrubbery.

8. A paper clip: part of a chain; finger nail cleaner; a hand toy (Rosato's students would have gotten this right immediately) ; a page marker.

9. A table spoon: sling shot; sand shovel (for use on a beach); musical instrument; eye cover during eye examination.

10. A hair brush: weapon; pretend microphone; back scratcher; drum stick.

How well did you do? People who are successful with this task are generally good with words and can do crossword puzzles well. Novelists and poets would also do well with this. Creative people who are also visionaries would do well on this test. On the other hand, practical people who are not risk-takers and who need a high standard of proof would probably not be successful on this test. Is this a test of intelligence? of creativity? or of personality? Yes, to all three.

6.2 INTELLIGENT UNDERSTANDING OF PROVERBS

Many people describe intelligence as "just common sense." Of course, if it is so common, why do so few people have it. This exercise tests your knowledge of common sense and what is known as social judgment, a concept frequently employed in tests of intelligence. You will be given a list of ten proverbs, some of which are common and others are more obscure. For each one, you will be asked to explain the meaning.

GOAL: To illustrate one way in which social judgment and common sense are measured on intelligence tests.

DIRECTIONS: Read each proverb and for each, answer the question :**What does this saying mean?** Concrete rephrasing of the proverb is not as cognitively demanding as determining an abstract meaning.

1. Absence makes the heart grow founder.

2. Actions speak louder than words.

3. A bad workman blames his tools.

4. A bleating sheep loses a bite.

5. Blood is thicker than water.

6. Conscience makes cowards of us all.

7. There is no use crying over spilt milk.

8. Give a dog a bad name and hang him.

9. What can you expect from a pig but a grunt.

10. Stupid is as stupid does (From the movie and novel Forrest Gump).

Possible interpretations (don't peek!)

1. You don't know what you've got till it's gone (Joanie Mitchell). When away, the person is missed more than one might realize.

2. Judge a person (particularly a politician) by what the person does rather than by what is said.

3. Clothes may not make the person and tools alone don't make the carpenter. Someone who is mechanically challenged (P.C. for a klutz) will blame the hammer rather than the holder.

4. A person who spends too much time talking about acting frequently misses the opportunity for action, also known as "paralysis by overanalysis."

5. Family is more critical than friends. Of course that depends upon one's family and upon one's friends. (We don't necessarily agree with these but we're here to show you what they mean.)

6. This is from that great psychologist who is missing from section one: William Shakespeare. Thinking about our actions and how they might impact on others often changes the way we behave. (The politicians to whom we referred to in item 2 should read this proverb and take it to heart.)

7. "Don't send good money after bad" is the companion to this proverb. Once an event has occurred and one no longer has control over it, forget about it and get on with life. Worrying and trying to make a bad situation better frequently results in more troubles.

8. This proverb deals with the importance of character and reputation. Once sullied, a person's ability to get on with life is extremely difficult. Parolees face this problem.

9. People who engage in boorish behavior on a regular basis have so tarnished their reputation that boorishness is expected from them.

   (Proverbs 8 & 9 make an interesting tandem. The former implies an unfair ruining of one's reputation and how that will follow the person for life; the latter implies that behavior is so regular that it's inappropriateness becomes expected. Who is to decide which is correct for any given individual? That is part of social judgment.)

10. Individuals are stupid not because someone says so (a variation of the "Sticks and stones" limerick) but by their actions. Once again, refer back to item two.

SCORING:

In our opinion, items three, four, six, eight, nine, and ten are more difficult than the others. Therefore, if you got all of the others correct and at least half of the difficult ones right, you can conclude that your social judgment is average or above. But remember, proverbs are only valuable if the advice they give is valid-and put to good use. No matter how you scored on this quiz about proverb <u>knowledge</u>, it is your ability to <u>act</u> effectively in social situations that counts most in life.

6.3 WORD PAIRS

Tests of intelligence often rely upon the measurement of verbal concept formation which is presented in the form of analogies. Verbal concept formation requires the individual to determine the how words are related, that is, into which category the words belong. For example, an orange and a tangerine belong in the category of fruit. However, an even higher level of categorization would yield the response that an orange and a tangerine are both citrus fruits.

The exercise below gives you the opportunity to test your level of verbal concept formation.

GOAL: To illustrate how verbal concept formation is measured on tests of cognitive ability.

DIRECTIONS: Read each word pair and write in the space provided the way in which the word pair is related. Each pair will have a good answer and a better answer.

In what way are : _______ and : _______ related:

1. puppy kitten ______________________________
2. coat jacket ______________________________
3. nose mouth ______________________________
4. sofa bed ______________________________
5. Spring Fall ______________________________
6. pool lake ______________________________
7. tulip bulb peach pit ______________________________
8. fax machine walkie talkie ______________________________
9. ice steam ______________________________
10. start finish ______________________________

Sample Answers:

	Good	Better
1.	animals, pets	animals at young age
2.	clothing	outer clothing
3.	parts of face	senses
4.	furniture	used for sleeping
5.	time of year	seasons
6.	contain water	recreational sites
7.	part of plant/vegetation	beginning of life
8.	machines	communication devices
9.	result from temperature change	change in status of water
10.	beginning and end	terminal points

SCORING:

The "better" answers are those which require a higher order of thinking in that the degree of the relationship is more specific. A reasonably good score would be to have at least six or seven of the "better" answers and no more than one incorrect answer. Of course, our goal is not to test your verbal concept formation but rather to illustrate how it is done on intelligence tests.

6.4 WATER, WATER EVERYWHERE

The problems which follow are ones which are designed to demonstrate your problem solving ability, a component of many intelligence tests.

GOAL: To determine how good of a problem solver you are and to demonstrate the advantage and disadvantage of a response set.

DIRECTIONS: In each item, you have an unlimited supply of water, empty containers in the sizes listed (with no markings on the containers except the size), and a need to return with the exact amount of requested water. As in most standardized tests, the items are arranged in order of difficulty.

The first three items are relatively easy and each should be solved within 45 seconds; the next three are moderately difficult and each should be solved within 75 seconds; the final ones are designed to make your hair hurt! (but should take no more than two minutes each.)

Container # 1	Container #2	Container #3	Amount of Water Needed
1. 10 quarts	7 quarts		3 quarts
2. 22 quarts	3 quarts		16 quarts
3. 18 quarts	3 quarts	1 quart	14 quarts
4. 32 quarts	4 quarts	3 quarts	22 quarts
5. 14 quarts	11 quarts	10 quarts	13 quarts
6. 10 quarts	29 quarts	4 quarts	11 quarts
7. 32 quarts	4 quarts	3 quarts	34 quarts
8. 18 quarts	43 quarts	10 quarts	5 quarts
9. 13 quarts	84 quarts	5 quarts	8 quarts

Solutions:

The first three items are basic subtraction problems. For the first problem, fill the 10 quart container, pour it into the 7 quart container and the remainder (in the 10 quart container) is 3 quarts. The second problem requires you to fill the 22 quart container and to twice pour water into the 3 quart container. This will leave 16 quarts in the 22 quart container. The third item is similar to the second (thus illustrating the importance of a response set). Water from the filled 18 quart container is to be poured into the 3 quart container and into the 1 quart container, leaving exactly 14 quarts in the 18 quart container. (We told that these would be easy.)

Item 4 is a bit more difficult. However, the same process which was used in item 3 can be applied here. The 32 quart container is filled and then poured into the 4 quart container (leaving 28 quarts). Next, 3 more quarts are put into the 3 quart container (leaving 25 quarts); this process is repeated again so that exactly 22 quarts are left in the 32 quart container.

As you saw, a pattern of thinking (or a response set) has developed. You start by filling the largest container and proceed to pour a portion into one or more of the smaller containers until you are left with the exact amount requested. However, sometimes the reliance on a response set can be stifling to our thinking and a shift in focus is required. Item 5 makes such a demand. The 14 quart container is still filled first. Then the water is poured into the 11 quart container. This leaves 3 quarts in the 14 quart container; 11 quarts are in the next container and the 10 quart container is empty. At this point, you could have filled the 10 quart container from the water supply and added that amount to the 3 quarts in the 14 quart container. A more parsimonious method (in terms of saving water) would be to empty the water from the 11 quart container into the 10 quart container and then combine that with the water in the 14 quart container. (This item requires addition as well as subtraction.

Item 6 requires you to start by filling the second container (the 29 quart container). This would be poured into the 10 quart container (leaving 19 quarts). Next, the water from that container is twice poured into the 4 quart container until 11 quarts remain in the 29 quart container.

The last three items are the most difficult (or are they?) Item 7 requires addition and subtraction. The 32 quart container is poured into the 4 quart container (28 quarts are left). The 3 quart container is then filled twice; one time it is emptied into the 32 quart container (31 quarts now in that one) and the other time it remains in the container. Thus, to solve this problem, two containers (the 32 quart container which has 31 quarts and the 3 quart container which is filled) are needed.

Item 8 is easily solved when you think about numbers. When 18 is subtracted from 43, the remainder is 25. The 10 quart container can be filled twice from the 25 quarts remaining in the 43 quart container. Thus, the amount left in the largest container is 5 quarts.

The final item is difficult only if your response set does not allow you to make shifts. All of the previous items required that you use all of the provided information. Item 9 is solvable by ignoring the 84 quart container. When the contents of the 13 quart container are poured into the 5 quart container, 8 quarts are left in the 13 quart container.

Were items 7 through 9 more difficult or were they easier? Your response would depend on your ability to learn from the previous problems. That is, if item 8 were the first problem you were asked to solve, it would have taken you longer to do so than it would have after you solved the first 7 problems. You can probably demonstrate this with a simple experiment. Give one group of your friends the first 8 items in the order presented. Calculate the time it took to solve item 8. Then, to a different group of friends, just give item 8 and calculate the time. Our guess (hypothesis) is that the group which only had item 8 will take longer for that problem than would the group which had the experience of solving items 1 through 7.

SCORING:

0 - 3 Correct: Water Carrier Level

4 - 6 Correct: River of Dreams Level

7 - 9 Correct: Oceans of Possibility Level

In youth we learn, in age we understand.
Ebner Eschenbach

Middle Age is when you have met so many people
that every new person
reminds you of someone else and usually is.
Ogden Nash

I am old enough to see how little I have done in so much time,
and how much I have to do in so little.
Sheila Kaye-Smith

You've heard of the three ages of life--youth, age, and "you're looking wonderful."
Francis Cardinal Spellman

7

SECTION SEVEN: HUMAN DEVELOPMENT

Human growth across the life span is an exciting topic. Each of us experiences it from different perspectives even as all of us begin life as dependent infants. We learn about infancy and childhood both by living it and by observing others in their own journeys. Developmental processes can be understood if they are studied, through systematic observation. People who spend thoughtful time with infants, children, adolescents, adults, and the aging have the best opportunity to truly learn about these processes. Before you begin to study development, however, you must know some things about yourself: your own attitudes towards having and raising children, what you consider important in children's school experiences, and how you feel about the aged--and about your own eventual aging.

The exercises in this section represent a journey through the our own change process--the life cycle. We start out with adulthood, contemplating procreation. That is, we ask you to look at some factors which are important before deciding whether or not to bring a child into the world. Assuming that the decision was made to have a child, we next ask you to look at your attitudes toward raising a child. Next, you will be asked to assess your attitudes toward the aging. Finally we end by looking at your developmental motivation towards school and work.

This section is designed for introspection and empathy. That is, look inside yourself and simultaneously see what it is like to be a different age. Hopefully, you'll learn a little bit more about yourself and understand others a bit better.

Human Development exercises include:

7.1 Assessing Readiness to Become a Parent
7.2 Anders Child Rearing Attitude Scale
7.3 Attitudes Towards Aging
7.4 How's Your Academic Motivation?

7.1 ASSESSING YOUR READINESS TO BECOME A PARENT

Many factors have to be taken into account when one is considering parenthood. What follows are some questions which should be asked and some issues which should be considered before making this decision. Some issues are relevant to both men and women; others apply only to women. There are no "right" or "wrong" answers.

GOAL: To help determine your attitude about parenting.

DIRECTIONS: For each item in each category, check "yes' or "no".

YES NO

Physical Health

___ ___ 1. Are you in reasonably good health (physically)?

___ ___ 2. Do you have any behaviors or conditions that could be of special concern?

___Obesity	___Anemia
___Smoking	___Diabetes
___Drug Use	___Sexually Transmitted Diseases
___Hypertension	___Epilepsy
___Previous Pregnancy or Delivery Problems	___Prenatal Exposure to DES (if so you know what this is)

___ ___ 3. Are you presently under 20 or over 35 years of age?

___ ___ 4. Do you or does your partner have a family history of a genetic problem that a baby might inherit?

___Hemophilia	___Phenylketonuria (PKU)
___Sickle Cell Anemia	___Cystic Fibrosis
___Down Syndrome	___Thalassemia
___Tay-Sachs Disease	___Other

Financial Circumstances

___ ___ 1. Do you have health insurance, and if so will it cover the costs of pregnancy, prenatal tests, delivery, and medical attention for mother and baby before and after the birth?

YES NO

___ ___ 2. Can you afford the supplies for the baby: diapers, bedding, crib, stroller, car seat, clothing, food, and medical supplies?

___ ___ 3. Will one parent leave her/his job to care for the baby?

___ ___ 4. If so, can the decrease in family income be worked into the family budget?

___ ___ 5. If both parents will continue to work, has affordable child care been set up?

___ ___ 6. The first few years of raising a baby can cost $10,000; can you save and/or provide the necessary money?

Education, Career, and Child Care Plans

___ ___ 1. Have you completed as much education as you want?

___ ___ 2. Have you sufficiently established yourself in a career, if that is important to you?

___ ___ 3. Have you investigated parental leave and company-sponsored child care?

___ ___ 4. Do both parents agree on child care arrangements?

Lifestyle and Social Support

___ ___ 1. Would you be willing to give up the freedom to do what you want to do when you want to do it?

___ ___ 2. Would you be willing to restrict your social life, to miss lost leisure time and privacy?

___ ___ 3. Would you and your partner be prepared to spend more time at home? Would you have enough time to spend with a child?

___ ___ 4. Are you prepared to be a single parent if your partner leaves or dies?

___ ___ 5. Do you have a network of family and friends who will help you with the baby? Are there community resources you can call on for additional assistance?

YES NO

Readiness

___ ___1. Are you prepared to have a helpless being completely dependent on you 24 hours a day?

___ ___2. Do you like children? Have you enough experiences with babies, toddlers, and teenagers?

___ ___3. Do you think time spent with children is time well spent?

___ ___4. Do you communicate easily with others?

___ ___5. Do you have enough love to give a child? Can you express affection easily?

___ ___6. Do you feel good enough about yourself to respect and nurture others?

___ ___7. Do you have safe ways of handling anger, frustration, and impatience?

___ ___8. Would you be willing to devote a great part of your life, at least 18 years, to being responsible for a child?

Relationship with Your Partner

___ ___1. Do you have a partner who wants to have a child? Are they committed both to you and to becoming a parent? Is he or she willing to answer these same questions?

___ ___2. Have you both discussed long and thoroughly your reasons for wanting a child?

___ ___3. Does either of you have philosophical objections to adding to the world's population?

___ ___4. Have you and your partner discussed each other's feelings about religion, work, family, and child raising? Are your feelings compatible and conducive to good parenting?

___ ___5. Would both you and your partner contribute in raising the child?

___ ___6. Is your relationship stable? Could you provide a child with a really good home environment?

YES NO

___ ___ 7. After having a child, would your partner and you be able to separate if you should have unsolvable problems? Would you feel obligated to remain together for the sake of the child?

Scoring/Interpretation (by Donovan and Rosato):

Unlike many of the other exercises in the book which look on the lighter side of psychology, this task is serious stuff. Hopefully, even if you are not ready to make the decision of becoming a parent at this time, you would have gained some insight into the issues that a new parent must face. Additionally, you might also realize now what a parent of a newborn goes through. Being a parent is a, if not the, most rewarding and demanding role. Preparation will not guarantee that your experience will be free of conflict and pain, but by examining your resources and constraints, you can enter the decision about whether to become a parent with acceptance and hope.

7.2 ANDERS CHILD REARING ATTITUDE SCALE

What are your attitudes toward child rearing? The exercise that follows was originally developed as a part of a research project involving institutional personnel who work with children.

GOAL: To assess your attitude toward child rearing.

DIRECTIONS: For each item, place a check next to the statement you believe to most correct. Choose only one statement per item. For now, ignore the letters in parentheses.

I. INFANCY AND EARLY CHILDHOOD

1. The feeding of an infant or small child should be:
   ___at the convenience of the mother (C)
   ___at a definite and regular time (B)
   ___whenever he/she wants it (A)

2. If a baby cries when he is neither hurt, wet, or hungry, I believe:
   ___he should be left to cry (B)
   ___he should be picked up (A)

3. A child should be weaned:
   ___before nine months (D)
   ___between nine and 18 months (C)
   ___before two years (B)
   ___anytime she seems ready (A)

4. A child should be toilet trained:
   ___as soon as possible (D)
   ___before 12 months (C)
   ___between 12 and 24 months (B)
   ___anytime he seems ready (A)

5. A child should stop wetting the bed:
   ___between two and three years (D)
   ___between four and five years (C)
   ___by school age (B)
   ___anytime she seems ready (A)

Source: Used with permission of the author, Dr. Sarah Frances Anders, Louisiana College, Pineville, Louisiana.

6. A child who wets the bed should:
   ___be taken to the doctor (D)
   ___be physically punished (C)
   ___be scolded (B)
   ___be ignored (A)

7. Thumb sucking in children should:
   ___stop by five or six years (D)
   ___be physically punished (C)
   ___be investigated (B)
   ___be ignored (A)

8. An infant/small child needs a great deal of affection and personal care; I:
   ___strongly agree (A)
   ___agree somewhat (B)
   ___disagree somewhat (C)
   ___strongly disagree (D)

9. A person should have his own room and bed:
   ___from birth (A)
   ___by school age years (B)
   ___between ages six and 12 (C)
   ___by teen years (D)

10. Children should usually be seen and not heard; I:
    ___strongly agree (D)
    ___agree somewhat (C)
    ___disagree somewhat (B)
    ___strongly disagree (A)

11. Imaginative play should not be encouraged, because this leads to lying in later years; I:
    ___strongly agree (D)
    ___agree (C)
    ___disagree somewhat (B)
    ___strongly agree (A)

II. CHILDHOOD AND PRE-PUBERTY

1. Physical punishment is necessary; I:
   ___strongly agree (D)
   ___agree somewhat (C)
   ___disagree somewhat (B)
   ___strongly disagree (A)

2. If a child masturbates, I believe that he should be:
   ___punished severely (D)
   ___told that it's dirty (C)
   ___ignored (B)
   ___allowed to do it (A)

3. A child should be permitted to make some decisions for herself:
   ___before school age (A)
   ___between ages six and nine (B)
   ___between ages nine and 12 (C)
   ___during early teen years (D)

4. A child should be allowed to watch television:
   ___never (C)
   ___with definite restrictions (B)
   ___whenever he wants to (A)

5. Children should be assigned appropriate household task to do; I:
   ___strongly agree (D)
   ___agree somewhat (C)
   ___disagree somewhat (B)
   ___strongly disagree (A)

6. A child should be severely punished for lying; I:
   ___strongly agree (D)
   ___agree somewhat (C)
   ___disagree somewhat (B)
   ___strongly disagree (A)

7. It's perfectly normal for children to sometimes take things that belong to others; I:
   ___strongly agree (A)
   ___agree somewhat (B)
   ___disagree somewhat (C)
   ___strongly disagree (D)

8. If you leave them alone, children will grow out of imaginary friends; I:
   ___strongly agree (A)
   ___agree somewhat (B)
   ___disagree somewhat (C)
   ___strongly disagree (D)

9. It's perfectly normal for young boys to be fighting all the time; I:
   ___strongly agree (D)
   ___agree somewhat (C)
   ___disagree somewhat (B)
   ___strongly disagree (A)

10. When a child is sick, he should still be expected to be well-behaved and obedient; I:
   ___strongly agree (D)
   ___agree somewhat (C)
   ___disagree somewhat (B)
   ___strongly disagree (A)

SCORING:

Review (but **do not change**) your answers for each section separately. Every "D" selected is to be multiplied by a -2; every "C" selected is to be multiplied by -1; every "B" selected is to be multiplied by +1; and every "A" selected is to be multiplied by +2. The range of scores for each section is: Infancy and Early Childhood (-19 to +22); Childhood and Pre-Puberty (-19 to +20). The range for the total instrument is (-38 to +42).

ANALYSIS and INTERPRETATION:

Positive scores are more indicative of a permissive or child oriented attitude toward child rearing while negative scores indicate a more restrictive and more adult oriented attitude. It would be instructive for you to see if your attitude changed as the age of the child changed. That is, are you more or less permissive with a toddler than a child? Scores which total close to zero can be seen as either balanced or may result from shifts in attitude depending on age or other factors.

(Note: This scoring and interpretation is based upon but is not a complete replication of Dr. Ander's work. Some minor changes were made in the wording of some of her original items and some modifications made in the assignment of values to the items.)

Did You Know That...

For centuries, there has been a debate about whether parents should allow their greater freedom (permissiveness) or to be authoritative with them (restrictiveness). The argument for permissivenes is that it tends to foster the inculcation of societal values for their own sake. (Something is wrong, regardless of whether or not one gets caught.) Restrictiveness is viewed as necessary to deliver appropriate consequences for behavior. Which is correct? Both and neither. Some children thrive in a permissive environment; others cannot handle the freedom. Some children rebel in an authoritative home, especially if not perceived as loved; others see restriction as support and needed structure. While there are no right or wrong absolutes, extremism in either direction can be detrimental to the child.

7.3 ATTITUDES ABOUT AGING AND THE ELDERLY

Most of us have little real understanding of what it is like to grow older or what our lives will be like as we age. This exercise is designed to test how well you truly know life's journey.

GOAL: To increase your understanding of the elderly.

DIRECTIONS: For each of the following questions circle T for True and F for False.

1. T F Most people over age 65 have little interest in sexual relations.
2. T F Our ability to see and hear grows weaker as we age.
3. T F Most people over age 65 live in a nursing home.
4. T F People today can expect to live longer than ever before.
5. T F Physical strength grows weaker as we age.
6. T F There is little we can do to slow down the rate at which our bodies age.
7. T F Women live longer than men do.
8. T F Most older people are just not able to learn new skills.
9. T F Most older people are depressed most of the time.
10. T F People tend to go to church more often as they age.
11. T F Most older people cannot wait to retire.
12. T F Older people are more likely to have mental problems than younger or middle aged folks.
13. T F Older people are less likely to try new things and take risks.
14. T F Most people over age 65 do not live with their children.
15. T F All of our bodies organs age at the same rate.
16. T F The median age of the population is increasing.
17. T F As our population ages we can expect crime rates to decline.
18. T F Most people over age 65 are socially isolated and lonely.
19. T F The reaction times of older people are slower than for younger people.
20. T F There is little that can be done to prevent memory loss as we age.

SCORING:

The following questions are True: 2, 4, 7, 14, 16, 17, 19, the remainder are False. Some facts:

1. Most healthy people who are part of a couple continue having satisfying sexual relations well into their 70s and 80s.
3. Only about 10% of the elderly require some form of institutional care.
5. Use it or lose it. With good diet and eating habits, our muscle tone may decline only a percentage point or two per year.
6. See the answer to number 5.
8. While learning may take a bit longer, the ability to learn is unchanged.
9. The elderly are no more or less likely to be depressed than people of any age.
10. Church attendance peaks in middle age and actually declines slightly with growing older.
11. Actually, people who enjoy their work are in no hurry to end it.
12., 15, and 20. See the answer to number 9.
13. Nope.
18. Nope, for most people over 65, they are only as lonely and isolated as the life they created for themselves when they were younger.

What it means:

If you scored 16 or more correct you are doing better than average for people of any age. 12 to 15 correct is not bad, while 8-11 is only so-so. Actually, if you got less than half right you are in for some rude shocks as you grow older. As a famous quote goes, "If I'd known I was going to use this body for this long, I would have taken better care of it."

For More Information On... the elderly, contact any of the following agencies:

American Association of Retired Persons
National Gerontology Resource Center
1909 K Street, NW
Washington DC 20049 202- 728-4880

Andrus Gerontology Center
University of Southern California
Los Angeles, Ca 90089
213-743-6060

American Society on Aging
833 Market Street, Suite 516
San Francisco, Ca 94103
415-743-2617

Self-Help for the Elderly
640 Pine Street
San Francisco, Ca 94108
415-982-9171

Additionally, every state has an office/commission on aging.

7.4 HOW'S YOUR ACADEMIC MOTIVATION?

This questionnaire looks at how you view school and school work at this point in your development. There are no right or wrong answers. Just tell how you feel by darkening only one response for each question.

	YES!	Yes	??	No	NO!
Example: Do you like music?	☐	☐	☐	☐	☐

GOAL: To ascertain what factors you believe influence your academic performance.

DIRECTIONS: Darken the square under **YES!** if you really love music; **Yes** if you kind of like music; **??** if you are not sure; **No** if you do not like music very much; and **NO!** if you hate music.
Now answer all the questions below.

		YES!	Yes	??	No	NO!
1.	Do your grades or marks get worse when you do not work hard?	☐	☐	☐	☐	☐
2.	Does studying before a test seem to help you get a higher score?	☐	☐	☐	☐	☐
3.	Do your grades or marks stay about the same no matter how hard you study?	☐	☐	☐	☐	☐
4.	Do your lowest grades or marks come about when you do not study for a test?	☐	☐	☐	☐	☐
5.	Do you think studying for a test is a waste of time?	☐	☐	☐	☐	☐
6.	Do your grades or marks get better when you do your homework carefully?	☐	☐	☐	☐	☐
7.	Do you have much control over the grades or marks you get?	☐	☐	☐	☐	☐

SOURCE: Reprinted with the permission of Margaret M. Clifford, Department of Educational Psychology, University of Iowa.

		YES!	Yes	??	No	NO!
8.	When you do worse than usual do you feel it is your fault?	☐	☐	☐	☐	☐
9.	When a teacher gives you a low grade or mark, it is because he/she does not like you?	☐	☐	☐	☐	☐
10.	When you really want a better grade or mark than usual, can you get it?	☐	☐	☐	☐	☐
11.	When you make up your mind to work hard, does your school work get better?	☐	☐	☐	☐	☐
12.	Do your test grades or marks go up when you study?	☐	☐	☐	☐	☐
13.	Is a high grade or mark just a matter of "luck" for you?	☐	☐	☐	☐	☐
14.	Do you think you deserve the grades or marks you get?	☐	☐	☐	☐	☐
15.	Do you usually get low grades or marks even when you study hard?	☐	☐	☐	☐	☐
16.	If you get a bad grade or mark, do you feel it is your fault?	☐	☐	☐	☐	☐
17.	Are tests just a lot of guesswork for you?	☐	☐	☐	☐	☐
18.	When you do poorly in school work, do you feel that you could have done better if you had wanted to?	☐	☐	☐	☐	☐

SCORING: Scores range from a low of 18 to a high of 95. For questions # 3,8,9,13,15, and 17, are scored 1 to 5 from left to right (that is a 1 for YES!, 2 for Yes, 3 for ??, 4 for No, and 5 for NO!). The remaining questions are scored 5 to 1 from left to right (that is 5 for YES!...1 for NO!). Write you score for each question next to the question then add up all the sums to get your total score. What it means (as interpreted by Donovan and Rosato): The higher your score, the more responsibility you accept for your own school results (and life in general). If you score 18-36 you are ready to blame anyone and anything other than yourself when things go wrong or right. A 37-56 leaves you sitting on the fence, sometimes you accept responsibility for your own actions but "Not Me" and "I Don't Know" are good friends of yours. If you score over 57, you not only talk the talk but you walk the walk. Nobody fools you and you don't try to fool yourself-your life is what you choose to make it.

8

SECTION EIGHT: MOTIVATION AND EMOTION

For most of us, we first enter the realm of psychology by asking why do people feel (and then act) the way they do. This "feeling" part of life is what psychologists refer to as motivation and emotions. Each of us is motivated by something. Some of us use a core set of values to guide our actions. Others look for more external reinforcers. Some strive to be the best there is. Others are committed to a certain activity and become almost "addicted" to it. Finally, some of us are driven by the desire to be perfect.

The exercises in section eight explore each of the possibilities above. The first exercise lists 18 items which people tend to value. You are asked to rank them and then to compare your scores with a national sample. The third task is even more introspective. You are asked to evaluate each of 25 items on a scale of one to five. Hopefully, you will learn to use your own reinforcers to become more productive. The fourth exercise is a self improvement one; it suggests ways for you to reach self-actualization. Commitment to physical activity and sport is the theme of the fifth task. Finally, we look at the downside to motivation. Unrealistic demands of perfectionism can lead to negative emotions.

At the end of this section, you should know more about what you find reinforcing. Put that knowledge to use; in a sense, use it or lose it. Reinforcers at one age quickly lose their appeal later.

Motivation and emotion exercises include:

8.1 The Presence Of Values In Our Lives - How Values Guide Us
8.2 Self-Reinforcement as a Motivator
8.3 Be All That You Can Be: A User's Guide To Improving Self-Actualization
8.4 Commitment Wellness: Becoming Healthier And Happier
8.5 Assessment of Perfectionism

8.1 THE PRESENCE OF VALUES IN OUR LIVES- How Values Guide Us

The things in life which we value tend to motivate us. That is, we are generally more willing to put forth effort in order to get what we want out of life. This exercise asks you to look at what you value and subsequently to compare your values with those of a national sample.

GOAL: To determine what you value in life.

DIRECTIONS: Rank order the list of values below in terms of how important they are as guiding principles in your life. Assign a rank of **1** to the value that is the **most important** guiding principle in your life and a rank of **18** to the one that is the **least important**.

_____A Comfortable Life

_____An Exciting Life

_____A Sense of Accomplishment

_____A World at Peace

_____A World of Beauty

_____Equality

_____Family Security

_____Freedom

_____Happiness

_____Inner Harmony

_____Mature Love

_____National Security

_____Pleasure

SOURCE: Reprinted by permission from pages 138 and 139 of *Adjustment and Competence: Concepts & Applications* by Grasha and Kirschenbaum;

_____Salvation

_____Self-Respect

_____Social Recognition

_____True Friendship

_____Wisdom

Part 2. How would you answer the following questions?

In what ways do your rankings agree or disagree with how other people rank each value?

Did you have as large a difference between how you ranked freedom and equality as did the people in the national survey? If you did, does this mean that you are more interested in your personal freedom than you are for other people?

Research reveals that the equality rankings of people but not the freedom rankings had a lot to do with attitudes toward racism. The higher people ranked equality, the more favorable their attitudes were towards civil rights issues and the more anti-racist was their behavior (Rokeach, Rokeach, & Grube, 1984). If you ranked equality as less important freedom, does this mean you not are as concerned about civil rights and racism?

How did you rank the value "a world of beauty"? The Rokeach study showed that eleven year olds rank it seventh, fifteen year olds, fourteenth, and adults put it at seventeenth on the list. If you ranked it as less important, what does that mean? Do you think that people are becoming less interested in the environment? If you ranked it as unimportant, are you also not interested in protecting the environment?

Now pretend that you are visiting a mysterious, beautiful, and exotic country. One day while visiting a local market, you are attracted to a tent marked "value exchange". You enter to find that people are trading their values with one another. No one can leave unless they trade one of their values for one or more new ones. You are asked to pick one of your values from the list above to trade and to indicate what new value you would want in return. What would you say?

SCORING:

Part 1. Compare your responses to a national sample.

The degree to which each of the values listed below were important guiding principles in the lives of people is shown. The data are from a national survey of the importance of values in the lives of American men and women from Rokeach, S. J., Rokeach, M. & Grube, J. W. (1984, November). "The great American values test." *Psychology Today.*

VALUE	NATIONAL RANKING
A Comfortable Life	8
An Exciting Life	17
A Sense of Accomplishment	7
A World at Peace	2
A World of Beauty	15
Equality	12
Family Security	1
Freedom	3
Happiness	5
Inner Harmony	11
Mature Love	14
National Security	13
Pleasure	16

Salvation	10
Self-Respect	4
Social Recognition	18
True Freedom	9
Wisdom	6

8.2 SELF-REINFORCEMENT AS A MOTIVATOR

What motivates you? That is, what types of satisfying "desserts" will cause you to eat your spinach? Do you study to get good grades? To get praise from a significant other? To get tuition reimbursement? To avenge the teacher/counselor who denigrated your ability? Each of us is motivated (or reinforced) by some external factor(s).

GOAL: To identify the factors that motivate you and then use them to your advantage.

DIRECTIONS: Read each item below and rank it according to the following scale:

1 - not enjoyable to me

2 - minimally enjoyable to me

3 - somewhat enjoyable to me

4 - enjoyable to me

5 - WOW!!

1. Eating desserts (ice cream, cake etc.) ___

2. Eating a special meal or favorite treat. ___

3. Going to a favorite restaurant. ___

4. Drinking soft drinks (cola, punch, juice etc.) ___

5. Jogging ___

6. Walking alone ___

7. Exercising (aerobics, weight lifting etc.) ___

8. Playing video games___

9. Listening to music ___

1 - not enjoyable to me
4 - enjoyable to me
2 - minimally enjoyable to me
5 - WOW!!
3 - somewhat enjoyable to me

10. Reading newspapers ___

11. Reading magazines ___

12. Reading books ___

13. Watching television ___

14. Attending movies ___

15. Attending plays ___

16. Attending operas ___

17. Attending sporting events ___

18. Participating in sporting events ___

19. Bicycle/motorcycle riding ___

20. Engaging in outdoor activities (swimming, flying, hiking, camping, canoeing etc.) ___

21. Shopping ___

22. Sleeping ___

23. Performing (acting in plays, playing an instrument, painting, sculpturing etc.) ___

24. Participating in a hobby (building models, collecting stamps, photography etc.) ___

25. (You fill in this one) ____ ___

SCORING:

Look at all of the items which you ranked as 4 or 5. Use those activities (without breaking any federal, state, local, or college laws or policies) as motivators to get you to do things (like studying, completing these exercises, attending class etc.) which you might otherwise find aversive. The key is to do what you find unpleasant **before** rewarding yourself.

Take another look at your responses. Hopefully, there is some balance among the activities which you find enjoyable. You should get some pleasure from eating but you also need to develop other sources of fun. Likewise, if your preference is for the cerebral, then perhaps you need more physical activities. You may be able to trade swimming a mile for the privilege of reading a John Grisham novel, or vice versa.

For an extra eye-opener, compare your responses with those of your friends and classmates. Compare and contrast the differences between us all not just in the specific rewards we like but in the types of rewards overall such as having food highest, activities, etc.

A person who finds no satisfaction in themself,
seeks in vain for it elsewhere.
La Rouchefoucauld

As the softest clay in time becomes the hardest brick...a fragile leaf the diamond. As a stream of fiery ice freezes into unbending iron. As fleeting moments mount to millennia, too, may a man ascend to himself.
Shaolin Master Po

One finds one's way only by taking it.
A. D. Sertillanges

8.3 BE ALL THAT YOU CAN BE:

A USER'S GUIDE TO IMPROVING SELF-ACTUALIZATION

Some major theorists, Maslow and Rogers in particular, believe that people can be motivated by a desire to reach their maximum potential. The term used for that is self-actualization. Few of us ever reach that goal. However, all of us can try to improve.

GOAL: To provide some suggestions for improving your level of self-actualization.

DIRECTIONS: To improve your level of self-actualization, try the following.

1. Several times each day, sit down for a few minutes and try to identify your present feelings. Ask yourself: Am I tense? angry? comfortable? relaxed? peaceful? tired? frustrated?

2. After identifying your current feelings, try using them as a guide to your behavior. For example, if you feel tired, why not take a few minutes to rest? If you feel angry, why not find a constructive way to express that anger?

3. Keep a diary for a few weeks. Every few days write down a description of yourself. (We have included on the next page a daily diary sheet for you to copy and use for this.) Try to allow this description to vary as your feelings vary on the different days. Consider this question: Must I be the same on days when I feel different?

4. Try sharing some of your immediate experiences with a friend or two. Does doing this change the nature of your friendship? How does it affect your self confidence? Do your friends share their personal feelings with you? Or, do you always talk about things that have happened already or that will happen in the future?

Did You Know That...

Maslow conceptualized a self-actualized person as someone who utilizes his/her full capacity in doing what that person does best? Maslow's study identified the following individuals as having achieved self-actualization: Albert Einstein, Aldous Huxley, William James, Thomas Jefferson, Abraham Lincoln, Albert Schweitzer, and others.

SOURCE: Reprinted by permission from page 495 of *Adjustment and Competence: Concepts & Applications* by Grasha and Kirschenbaum;

Daily Diary

Time	Mood	Comments
		Wake up:

Today's Description of Me, Myself, and I:

8.4 COMMITMENT TO WELLNESS:

The Motivation to Become Healthier and Happier

Everyone who exercises has some degree of commitment to exercise or sport. "Addicted" runners probably feel very committed to jogging. People often envy that kind of commitment. They would like to increase their commitment or motivation to performing at their peak in a sport or to exercising more regularly than they currently do.

GOAL: To evaluate your present level of commitment to exercise or sport.

DIRECTIONS: How committed are you to improving your performance in your favorite sport or to exercise more frequently? Think of the sport in which you would most like to excel or the exercise activity that you would like to increase. Whenever you see the word BLANK in the questionnaire below, substitute the name of your sport or exercise. For example, Sarah wants to increase the number of times per week she swims twenty laps. When Sarah sees "_______" below, she should think, "swimming."

Read each of the ten items below. For each item, insert a number from one to five next to the item by deciding which of the following alternatives most accurately describes your current feelings about that item:

THE COMMITMENT QUESTIONNAIRE:

5 = extremely characteristic of me
4 = somewhat characteristic of me
3 = neither characteristic nor uncharacteristic of me
2 = somewhat uncharacteristic of me
1 = extremely uncharacteristic of me

_____ 1. I'm very committed to do ______.

_____ 2. I'm really eager to develop the kind of self-discipline I need to do ______.

_____ 3. I'm good at keeping my promise to do ______.

_____ 4. When I find ______ difficult to do, I try especially hard to stick with it.

SOURCE: Reprinted by permission from pages 336-337 of *Adjustment and Competence: Concepts & Applications* by Grasha and Kirschenbaum;

_____ 5. I will persist at ______ despite pain or discomfort.

_____ 6. Sometimes I push myself harder than I should when doing ______.

_____ 7. I am determined to reach my goals in ______.

_____ 8. I have gathered a lot of willpower to do ______.

_____ 9. I will persist at ______ despite occasional failures.

_____ 10. Regarding ______, I will not let myself down.

SCORING:

Sum your responses to the ten items on the Commitment Questionnaire. According to research by Rod Dishman and colleagues on a related questionnaire (Dishman, Ickes, & Morgan, 1980; Dishman & Ickes, 1981), you can interpret your scores as follows:

40 or more = a high degree of commitment
35 - 40 = a moderate degree of commitment
34 or less = a low degree of commitment

If this exercise showed you that your current commitment to exercise or sports is high, you are more likely to achieve your goals in those areas than is someone whose commitment score is low. Dishman and colleagues found that people who scored very high on a questionnaire like the Commitment Questionnaire worked harder and longer in various exercise and sport programs than did those who reported less commitment (Dishman, Ickes, & Morgan, 1980; Dishman & Ickes, 1981).

How could you increase your commitment to changing your exercise or sport participation? Since degree of commitment is determined by the importance of the goal, increasing commitment involves finding a way to increase the importance of the goals you pursue. Irving Janis and Leon Mann (1977) developed a very useful way to do this. They found that getting people to write out all of the likely consequences of pursuing and failing to pursue a goal can improve commitment to it.

8.5 ASSESSMENT OF PERFECTIONISM

Some people are not sure if they suffer from the unrealistic demands of perfectionism. Perfectionism may have become so much a part of their motivation that they no longer notice its effects.

The following assessment may help you become more aware of how perfectionism may be affecting your life. Use the following scale to measure your agreement or disagreement with the assessment statements. Try to respond to the way you usually think, feel, and behave.

GOAL: To determine how motivated you are to be perfect.

DIRECTIONS: Use the scale below to respond to each item.

+2 = Very much like me
+1 = Sometimes like me
0 = Neutral
-1 = Usually not like me
-2 = Definitely not like me

______ I should be able to excel at anything I attempt.

______ If I cannot do something really well, there is not point in doing it at all.

______ People will think less of me if I make mistakes.

______ If I do not set very high standards for myself, I will never be successful.

______ An average performance is unsatisfying to me.

______ If I get angry with myself for failing to live up to high standards, it will help me to do better in the future.

______ I should be upset when I make a mistake.

______ It is wrong to make the same mistakes several times.

______ I am less of a person when I fail at something important.

______ It is shameful when I display weakness or foolish behavior.

SOURCE: Reprinted by permission from page 66 of *Adjustment and growth in a Changing World* 3rd. edition by Napoli, Kilbride, and Tebbs;

SCORING:

Add up your score. My score is ______.

If your score is close to +20, you possess a very high degree of perfectionism. If your score is near -20, you are relatively unaffected by perfectionism. Scores in between reflect your relative closeness to these two extremes. This assessment has been used with several classes of college students. The results indicate that many of us tend to be affected, to varying degrees, by perfectionistic demands.

Did You Know That...

The authors (Napoli, Kilbride and Tebbs) believe that perfectionism arises out of unrealistic expectations which we put on ourselves. Curiously, however, these expectations have their genesis in childhood. Some common childhood experiences which could lead to perfectionism as an adult include, according to Napoli, et. al., the suppression of the urge to cry; the reification of our parents; subjugating personal needs for the wishes of others; and dissatisfaction with anything less than an A+ in all school work. So, chances are if you experienced one or more of these events, your score would be above 20.

9

SECTION NINE: CONSCIOUSNESS

Every day we experience different levels of awareness of our internal and external stimuli. Psychologists refer to these different levels as different states of consciousness. The most commonly studied states of consciousness include normal or waking consciousness, sleep, hypnosis, and the state produced by various consciousness-altering drugs.

Two of the most frequently asked questions of psychology students related to these topics are: "Can you psychoanalyze me?" and "Can you hypnotize me?" In this section, we can do nothing for the former, but we can at least give you some insight into the world of hypnotism.

We have excerpted some of the Harvard Group Scale of Hypnotic Susceptibility. We did this **not** to teach you how to hypnotize people but rather to show you how it is done and to allow you to possibly experience it under controlled, classroom, conditions.

The other exercises in this section assess your attitude toward the consciousness altering drug of marijuana and your overall addictability. Again, our expectations are that your experiences will be vicarious only.

Consciousness exercises include:

9.1 Harvard Group Scale of Hypnotic Susceptibility
9.2 Marijuana Attitude Scale
9.3 Rate Your Addictability

9.1 HARVARD GROUP SCALE OF HYPNOTIC SUSCEPTIBILITY

Note: The Harvard Group Scale of Hypnotic Susceptibility by Ronald E. Shor and Emily Carata Orne is an adaptation for group administration with self-report scoring of the original, individually administered and objectively scored Stanford Hypnotic Susceptibility Scale which was developed by Weitzenhoffer and Hilgard in 1959. The adapted scale was developed to eliminate the need for a trained examiner. What follows is an abridged adaptation of that scale.

Hypnotism is being used more and more by physicians: for example, by dentists to relieve pain, by obstetricians to make childbirth easier, by psychiatrists to reduce anxiety. If the process can be understood, more will be known about the relationship between ideas and action, more will also be known about the way personality operates.

There are, of course, social and ethical considerations regarding hypnosis. There are occasional disturbances which may arise from the hypnotic experience. Generally, according to the authors of this scale, two or three percent of the individuals experienced some level of disturbance. "In some cases a disturbance such as a headache resulted from the revival under hypnosis of bad childhood experiences under chemical anesthetics; in other cases the disturbance attributed to hypnosis could be shown to have been there prior to the hypnotic induction. While hypnosis is in general entirely harmless, and often helpful, the assumption must not be made that it is a trivial experience. For some subjects it is a deep intrusion into their private lives. Hence the person planning experiments on hypnosis should be prepared for the possibility of some unusual consequences." (Weitzenhoffer, A. M. & Hilgard, E. R. 1959, *Stanford Hypnotic Susceptibility Scale.* p. 6 Palo Alto: Consulting Psychologists Press).

PARTICIPATION IN THIS PROCEDURE IS VOLUNTARY ON YOUR PART. The procedure works best when one person reads the instructions to the other. Each party should implicitly trust the other. Therefore it is recommended that *YOUR PROFESSOR* or other qualified individual lead you in this exercise. However, if that is not feasible, then you may read the instructions to your self to try to get an understanding of the steps used to hypnotize someone. An effort should be made to discourage a lack of seriousness in subjects and to prevent the presence of casual onlookers. Provisions should be made to prevent persons from entering the room once the procedure begins.

GOAL: To increase your understanding of hypnosis.

DIRECTIONS: You are agreeing to undergo a standard procedure for measuring susceptibility to hypnosis.

People experiencing hypnosis for the first time are sometimes a little uneasy because they do not know what the experience will be like, or because they may have a distorted notion of what it is like. It is very natural to be curious about a new experience.

To allow you to feel more fully at ease in the situation, please be assured of a few points. First of all, the experience, while a little unusual, may not seem so far removed from ordinary experience as you have been led to expect. Hypnosis is largely a question of your willingness to be receptive and responsive to ideas, and to allow these ideas to act upon you without interference. These ideas are called suggestions.

Second, you will not be asked to do anything that will make you look silly or stupid, or that will prove embarrassing to you. Hypnotism is serious science.

Third, and finally, there will be no probing into your personal affairs; there will be nothing personal about what you are to do or say during the hypnotic state.

Please make yourself comfortable in a chair. You should keep your glasses on but you might want to remove contact lenses.

Task 1. HEAD FALLING

[You may either have your professor read the instructions to you, or you may wish to read them to yourself to gain an understanding of the hypnotic induction procedures.]

To begin with, I want you to experience how it feels to respond to suggestions when you are not hypnotized. Please sit up straight in your chair....Close your eyes and relax; continue, however, to sit up straight. That's right. Eyes closed and sit up straight. Please stay in that position with your eyes closed, while at the same time letting yourself relax. [stay like this for 30 seconds]. Now just remain in the position and keep your eyes closed...sitting up straight in your chair...with your eyes closed.

In a moment I shall ask you to think of your head falling forward. As you know, <u>thinking</u> of a movement and <u>making</u> a movement are closely related. Soon after you <u>think</u> of your head falling you will experience a tendency to <u>make</u> the movement. You will find your head actually falling forward, more and more forward, until your head will fall so far forward that it will hang limply on your neck.

Listen carefully to what I say and think of your head falling forward, drooping forward. Think of your head falling forward, falling forward, more and more forward. Your head is falling forward, falling forward. More and more forward. Your head is falling more and more forward, falling more and more forward. Your head is going forward, drooping down, down, limp and relaxed. Your head is drooping, swaying, falling forward, falling forward, falling forward, falling, swaying, drooping, limp, relaxed, forward, forward, falling, falling, falling....Now!

That's fine. Now please sit up and open your eyes. That's right. Sit up and open your eyes. You can see how thinking about a movement produces a tendency to make the movement. You learn to become hypnotized as you bring yourself to give expression to your action tendencies. But at this point you have the idea of what it means to accept and act upon suggestions.

Task 2. EYE CLOSURE

Now I want you to seat yourself comfortably and rest your hands in your lap. That's right. Rest your hands in your lap. Now look at your hands and find a spot on either hand and just focus on it. It doesn't matter what spot you choose; just select some spot to focus on. I shall refer to the spot which you have chosen as the target. That's right...hands relaxed...look directly at the target. I am about to give you some instructions that will help you to relax and gradually to enter a state of hypnosis. Just relax and make yourself comfortable. I want you to look steadily at the target and while keeping your eyes upon it to listen to what I say. Your ability to be hypnotized depends partly on your willingness to co-operate and partly on your ability to concentrate upon the target and upon my words. You can be hypnotized only if you are willing. I assume that you are willing and that you are doing your best to co-operate by concentrating on the target and listening to my words, letting happen whatever you feel is going to take place. Just let it happen. If you pay close attention to what I tell you, and think of the things I tell you to think about, you can easily experience what it is like to hypnotized. There is nothing fearful or mysterious about hypnosis. It is a perfectly normal consequence of certain psychological principles. It is merely a state of strong interest in some particular thing. In a sense you are hypnotized whenever you see a good show and forget you are part of the audience, but instead feel you are part of the story. Many people report that becoming hypnotized feels at first like falling asleep, but with the difference that somehow or other they keep hearing my voice as a sort of background to whatever other experience they may have. In some ways hypnosis is like sleepwalking; however, hypnosis is also an individual experience and is not just alike for everyone. In a sense the hypnotized person is like a sleepwalker, for he can carry out various and complex activities while remaining hypnotized. All I ask of you is that you keep up your attention and interest and continue to cooperate as you have been cooperating. Nothing will be done that will cause you any embarrassment. Most people find this is a very interesting experience.

Just relax. Don't be tense. Keep your eyes on the target. Look at it as steadily as you can. Should your eyes wander away from it, that will be all right...just bring your eyes back to it. After a while you may find that the target gets blurry, or perhaps moves about, or again, changes color. That is all right. Should you get sleepy, that will be fine, too. Whatever happens, let it happen and keeping staring at the target for a while. There will come a time, however, when your eyes will be so tired, will feel so heavy, that you will be unable to keep them open any longer and they will close, perhaps quite involuntarily. When this happens, just let it take place.

As I continue to talk, you will find that you will become more and more drowsy. Not all people respond at the same rate to what I have to say. Some people's eyes will close before others.

Now just allow yourself to relax completely. Relax every muscle of your body. Relax the muscles of your legs...Relax the muscles of your arms....Relax the muscles of your hands....of your fingers...of your neck, of your chest....Relax all of the muscles of your body....Let yourself be limp, limp, limp, limp. Relax more and more. Relax completely, completely.

As you relax more and more, a feeling of heaviness comes over your body, to your legs and arms...into your whole body. Your breathing is becoming slow and regular, slow and regular. You are getting drowsy and sleepy, more and more drowsy and sleepy while your eyelids become heavier and heavier.

Your eyes are tired from staring. Soon you will not be able to keep your eyes open. Your eyes are tired from staring; your eyes are becoming wet from straining. You are becoming increasingly drowsy and sleepy. It would be so nice to close your eyes, to relax completely, relax completely. You will soon reach your limit. The strain will be so great, your eyes will be so tired, your lids will become so heavy, your eyes will close of themselves, close of themselves.

Your eyes may have closed by now, and if they have not, they would soon close of themselves. There is no need to strain them more.

Task 3. FINGER LOCK

Close your eyes and relax. Put your fingers together. Interlock your fingers together. Interlock your fingers and press your hands tightly together. That's it. Put your fingers together. Interlock your fingers and press your hands together. Interlock tightly...hands pressed tightly together. Notice how your fingers are becoming tightly interlocked together, more and more tightly interlocked...so tightly interlocked together that you wonder very much if you could take your fingers and hands apart...Your fingers are interlocked, tightly interlocked...and I want you to take your hands apart...just try...

Now, stop trying and relax. You notice how hard it was to get started to take them apart. Your hands are no longer tightly clasped together...You can take them apart. Now return your hands to their resting position and relax. Hands to their resting position and relax...just relax.

Task 4. COMMUNICATION INHIBITION

You are very relaxed now...deeply relaxed...think how hard it might be to communicate while so deeply relaxed...perhaps as hard as when asleep...I wonder if you could shake your head to indicate "no". I really don't think you could...You might try a little later to shake your head "no" when I tell you to...but I think you will find it quite difficult...Why don't you try to shake your head "no" now...just try to shake it. [Allow 10 seconds]

Stop trying and relax. You see again how you have to make an effort to do something normally as easy as shaking your head. You can shake it to indicate "no" much more easily now. Shake your head easily now...That's right, now relax. Just relax.

Task 5. HALLUCINATION (FLY)

I am sure that you have paid so close attention to what we have been doing that you have not noticed the fly which has been buzzing about you...But now that I call your attention to it you become increasingly aware of this fly which is going round and round about your head...nearer and nearer to you...buzzing annoyingly...hear the buzz getting louder as it keeps darting at you...You don't care much for this fly...You would like to shoo it away...get rid of it...It annoys you. Go ahead and get rid of it if want to...[Allow 10 seconds]

There, it's going away...it's gone...and you are no longer annoyed...no more fly. Just relax, relax completely. Relax...just relax.

Task 6. POST-HYPNOTIC SUGGESTION (TOUCHING LEFT ANKLE); AMNESIA

Remain deeply relaxed and pay close attention to what I am going to tell you next. In a moment I shall begin counting backwards from 20 to one. You will gradually wake up, but for most of the count you will still remain in the state you are now in. By the time I reach "five" you will open your eyes, but you will not be fully aroused. When I get to "one" you will be fully alert, in your normal state of wakefulness. You probably will have the impression that you have slept because you will have difficulty in remembering all the things I have told you and all the things you did or felt. In fact, you will find it to be so much of an effort to recall any of these things that you will have no wish to do so. It will be much easier simply to forget everything until I tell that you can remember. You will remember nothing of what has happened until I say to you: "Now you can remember everything.!" You will not remember anything until then. After you open your eyes, you will feel fine. You will have no headache or other after-effects. I shall now count backwards from 20, and at "five", not sooner, you will open your eyes but not be fully aroused until I say "one,". At "one" you will be awake...A little later you will hear a tapping noise like this [demonstrate a tapping noise here]. When you hear the tapping noise, you will reach down and touch your left ankle. You will touch your left ankle, but forget that I told you to do so, just as you will forget the other things until I tell you "Now you can remember everything." Ready, now: 20--19--18--17--16--15--14--13--12--11--10, half way--9--8--7--6--5--4--3--2--1. Wakeup! Wide awake! Any remaining drowsiness which you feel will quickly pass. [A distinct tapping, as demonstrated above, is now to be made. Pause for 10 seconds.]

Soon you will asked to turn the page and to begin writing your responses to questions. DO NOT TURN THE PAGE UNTIL INSTRUCTED TO DO SO. All right, now listen carefully to my words. *Now you can remember everything.* Please TURN THE PAGE NOW and follow the directions.

TESTING

Please write down now, briefly and in your own words, a *list* of the things that happened since you began looking at the target. Do not go into detail. Spend no more than three minutes on this.

On this page, write down a list of anything else that you now remember that you did not remember previously. Please do not go into detail. Spend no more than two minutes on this.

OBJECTIVE, OUTWARD RESPONSES

Listed below in chronological order are the six specific happenings which were suggested to you during the standard hypnotic procedure. We wish you to estimate whether or not you *objectively* responded to these six suggestions, that is, whether or not *an onlooker* would have observed that you did or did not make certain definite responses by certain specific, predefined criteria. In this section we are interested in your estimates of your *outward behavior* and *not* in what your *inner, subjective experience* of it was like. Later on you will be given an opportunity to describe your inner, subjective experience, but in this section refer only to the outward behavioral responses irrespective of what the experience may have been like subjectively.

It is understood that your estimates may in some cases not be as accurate as you might wish them to be and that you might even have to guess. But we want you to make whatever you feel to be your *best estimates* regardless.

Beneath a description of each of the six suggestions are sets of two responses, labeled A and B. Please *circle* either A or B for each question. Please answer every question.

1. HEAD FALLING

You were told to sit straight in your chair for 30 seconds and then to think of your head falling forward. Would you estimate that *an onlooker* would have observed that your head fell forward at least two inches during the time you were thinking about it happening?

Circle one: A. My head fell forward at least two inches.

B. My head fell forward less than two inches.

2. EYE CLOSURE

You were next told to rest your hands in your lap and pick out a spot on either hand as a target and concentrate on it. You were then told that your eyelids were becoming tired and heavy. Would you estimate that *an onlooker* would have observed that your eyelids had closed (before the time you were told to close them deliberately)?

Circle one: A. My eyelids had closed by then.

B. My eyelids had *not* closed by then.

3. FINGER LOCK

You were next told to interlock your fingers, told how your fingers would become tightly interlocked, and then told to try to take your hands apart. Would you estimate that *an onlooker* would have observed that your fingers were incompletely separated (before you were told to stop trying to take them apart)?

Circle one: A. My fingers were still incompletely separated by then.

B. My fingers had completely separated by then.

4. COMMUNICATION INHIBITION

You were next told to think how hard it might be to shake your head to indicate "no", and then told to try. Would you estimate that *an onlooker* would have observed you to make a recognizable shake of the head "no"? (That is, before you were told to stop trying.)

Circle one: A. I did *not* recognizably shake my head "no".

B. I did recognizably shake my head "no".

5. PERCEIVING THE FLY

You were next told to become aware of the buzzing of a fly which was said to become annoying, and then you were told to "shoo" it away. Would you estimate that *an onlooker* would have observed you make any grimacing, any movement, any outward acknowledgment of an effect (regardless of what it was like subjectively)?

Circle one: A. I did make some outward acknowledgment.

B. I did *not* make any outward acknowledgment.

6. POST-HYPNOTIC SUGGESTION (TOUCHING LEFT ANKLE)

You were next told that after you were awakened you would hear a tapping noise at which time you would reach down and touch your left ankle. You were further informed that you would do this but forget being told to do so. Would you estimate that *an onlooker* would have observed either that you reached down and touched your left ankle, or that you made any partial movement to do so?

Circle one: A. I made at least an observable partial movement to touch my left ankle.

B. I did *not* make even a partial movement to touch my left ankle, which would have been observable.

YOU MAY NOW REFER TO EARLIER PAGES- BUT PLEASE DO NOT WRITE ANYTHING FURTHER ON THEM.

INNER, SUBJECTIVE EXPERIENCES

Regarding the suggestion of PERCEIVING A FLY - how real was it to you? How vividly did you hear and feel it? Did you really believe at the time that it was there? Was there any doubt about its reality?

On the remainder of this page please describe any other of your inner, subjective experiences during the procedure which you feel to be of interest.

SCORING

Scoring is simply + for each item. The objective, behavioral items receive a + for every A response, a - for every B response. Amnesia is scores + if fewer than half of the items induced within hypnosis were recalled before the signal to remember was given. The items need not be mentioned by name to be counted, provided that it is reasonably clear which ones are meant. Each item can only count once, no matter how much detail is given.

INTERPRETATION (Extrapolated from Shor and Orne by Donovan and Rosato)

Individuals who have more than 4 + have a greater hypnotic susceptibility than those you have fewer than that number. Bear in mind that the above exercise was modified and abridged. Under other circumstances and settings, more susceptibility may be evidenced. An individual who appears relatively unsusceptible at this time by these standard procedures will not necessarily still be relatively unsusceptible at a later time or under different circumstances.

That you may retain your self-respect, it is better to displease the people by doing what you know is right, than to temporarily please them by doing what you know is wrong.
William J. H. Boetcker

One reason that I don't indulge is that I want to know when I am having a good time.
Lady Astor

9.2 MARIJUANA ATTITUDE SCALE

Marijuana falls into the category of a consciousness altering substance. Many individuals report that, after smoking marijuana, their perceptions of reality are changed. The following exercise allows you give your opinion on the use of marijuana.

GOAL: To ascertain your opinion of marijuana use.

DIRECTIONS: Use the scale below for each item.

1- Strongly Agree
2- Agree
3- Neutral
4- Disagree
5- Strongly Disagree

__ 1. Marijuana gives more pleasure than pain.

__ 2. Marijuana is not harmful to health.

__ 3. Marijuana should be legalized.

__ 4. The use of marijuana should not be considered a vice.

__ 5. Marijuana helps one cope with problems.

__ 6. Marijuana sharpens one's mind.

__ 7. Marijuana increases one's creativity.

__ 8. Marijuana use is a better drug than alcohol.

__10. People should not be prevented from using marijuana.

__11. Marijuana is one of life's greatest pleasures.

__12. Marijuana use should not be punished.

__13. Marijuana will continue to be popular in the future.

__14. Marijuana is not harmful.

__15. No one should be stopped from using marijuana.

__16. Marijuana helps one understand oneself.

__17. Marijuana is not related to other drug use.

SOURCE: Reprinted with the permission of the author, Dr. Daniel Baer, Boston College.

__18. Penalties are too severe for those who use marijuana.

__19. Marijuana induces passivity in a hostile world.

__20. Marijuana users are misunderstood.

SCORING:

If you scored below 30, you are probably are a candidate for membership in NORML (National Organization for Reform of Marijuana Laws); higher scores are indicative of more conservative views. (Of course, many of those who currently have those opinions used marijuana at a younger age; some inhaled, others did not.)

It is not likely that you were unaware of your attitudes prior to completing this checklist. The larger value may be in comparing your attitudes with other significant people in your life including your close relatives. It was a just a couple of generations ago the our great+ grandparents took many "potions" from their local druggist that contained marijuana, cocaine, even heroin and morphine.

Did You Know That...

Most adolescents do not and probably never will use marijuana? Fewer than 20% of high school seniors currently use marijuana. Some of the short-term effects of marijuana use include memory loss and difficulty with learning. Also, coordination is impaired and many experience an increased heart rate, with anxiety and possibly panic attacks. The coordination and depth perception needed for driving and other physical activities are also impaired. Research studies indicate that someone who smokes five joints per week may be taking in as many cancer-causing chemicals as someone who smokes a pack of cigarettes a day. People who use marijuana frequently develop the same kinds of breathing problems (frequent coughing, wheezing, more chest colds) as cigarette smokers do. Heavy marijuana use can delay puberty in males and can disturb female ovulation cycles. There is some research which found that babies born to marijuana users were shorter, weighed less, and had smaller head sizes than those born to mothers who did not use marijuana.

For More Information...

National Clearinghouse on Alcohol and Drug Information
P.O. Box 2345
Rockville, Md. 20847
1-800-729-6686.

(NOTE: Changes were made from the original items so that a Likert Scale could be created. Note also that the scoring and interpretation are solely Donovan and Rosato.)

9.3 RATE YOUR ADDICTABILITY

Each year hundreds of thousands of people in this country realize that they're addicted to something or other. And experts believe that all of us have the potential to become dependent on drugs, alcohol, shopping, even exercise. To find out if you're likely to get addicted to something, start concentrating and take this quiz.

GOAL: To determine your likeliness to become addicted

DIRECTIONS: Circle Yes or No as it applies to you

1. Is there something you would do absolutely anything for?

   Yes No

2. Have you ever done anything against your principles or against the law in order to be able to get something?

   Yes No

3. Are people continually telling you that you rely too much on certain things in your life?

   Yes No

4. When something goes wrong, do you often turn to one thing or activity to pick you up again?

   Yes No

5. Do you have secret activities that you do on a regular basis?

   Yes No

6. Do you have to triple-check things before you're satisfied?

   Yes No

7. Have you ever denied that you have a problem, even though you know that what you're doing isn't good for you?

   Yes No

8. Is there something in your life that you can't do without?

   Yes No

9. Do you feel compelled to do things that you know are not good for you?

   Yes No

10. Would you say you are usually able to cheer yourself up?

   Yes No

11. Is anyone in your family currently an addict or a rehabilitated addict?

   Yes No

SCORING:

1.	Yes	4	No	0	7.	Yes	2	No	0
2.	Yes	4	No	0	8.	Yes	4	No	0
3.	Yes	2	No	0	9.	Yes	3	No	0
4.	Yes	3	No	0	10.	Yes	0	No	2
5.	Yes	3	No	0	11.	Yes	5	No	0
6.	Yes	3	No	0					

Scoring Analysis and Interpretation:

27-35: Unfortunately this isn't the SAT test. A high score here could mean you are the type of person who is easily hooked. But the operative word is "could." So don't panic; but stand back and take a close look at your lifestyle! If you see anything that strikes you (or people you trust) as unhealthy or destructive (like getting drunk a lot, or smoking, or spending so much time on those talk lines that your parents take your phone away), try changing your habits and getting back under control. If you can't do it on your own (and many people can't, so don't be too hard on yourself), talk to the school nurse or your counselor about your problems, or explain the situation to your parents or your favorite aunt or whomever. Remember, you can ignore addictions. A lot of people do. But the problem won't just go away. And the longer you wait to deal with an addiction, the more damage is done and harder it will be to get better.

16-26: You've managed a pretty good balance between relying on yourself and relying on other things in your life. You know that if you hit a snag or feel depressed or whatever, you have two options: You're perfectly capable of picking yourself up and getting back on track that way, or you can call on trusted friends or occasional gimmicks (like treating yourself to a banana split or a window shopping spree) to do the trick. And that makes you pretty resistant to addictions. Just remember that no one is 100 percent immune.

0-15: You're one independent, self-sufficient, got-it-all-together kind of person. Great. Just don't be such a free spirit that you forget that people were meant to depend on other people and things to a certain extent. After all, no man or woman (including you) is an island. So the next time you're feeling a little weak in the knees (like when you fail that trig test or you have another fight with your boyfriend), go ahead and lean on a friend and let them cheer you up just this once. Or listen to your favorite song over and over again, or indulge in whatever healthy, nondestructive activity makes you happiest. Because a happy person is well on their way to dealing with just about any old thing.

It has been said that a man is three things:
what he thinks he is;
what others think he is;
and what he really is.
Which of these do you believe to be the truth?
Shaolin Master Kan

10

SECTION TEN: PERSONALITY

The exercises in this section, perhaps even more than in the others, will tell you about you. Most of us expect other people to demonstrate a certain level of consistency in their behaviors and beliefs across a variety of different situations and over long periods of time. The patterns found in these consistencies are what psychologists refer to as personality. In both behaviors or beliefs, the tasks in this section explore both of these manifestations.

The first exercise is one which we use with our students. You are asked to list some of the qualities which make you, you. Then, you are to ask a significant other to do the same about you. (Be careful who you pick.) The second exercise also requires the assistance of someone who knew you when. The exercise is designed to see how much, if at all, you have changed in terms of your temperament. You may be surprised at the results. In the third exercise you are asked to evaluate the aggressiveness of certain activities. Finally, we let you play another round of the matching game. This time we want you connect a personality theorist with her/his theory.

Your personality may not improve at the end of this section; however, your knowledge of yourself will. You may also learn something about your current and old friends and family members.

Personality exercises include:

10.1 Who Are You?
10.2 Personality And Temperament
10.3 Aggression? Says Who?
10.4 Personality Match Game

10.1 WHO ARE YOU?

What about you makes you, you? Trait theorists believe that enduring qualities like honesty, shyness, compulsiveness, define people. This exercise gives you the opportunity to look at your personal traits and then to have others look at you.

GOAL: To discover if others see you the same way that you see yourself

DIRECTIONS: First, list below the five to seven enduring traits which you believe best describe you. Second, ask a person who is very close to you now to do the same for you. Third, ask someone who knew you as a child (a parent/guardian, sibling) to do the same. Finally, compare the lists.

Traits as I see myself:

____

____

____

____

____

____

____

Interpretation:

If you are honest, and if the other people who are working with you on this task know/knew you well enough, then there should be a high degree of overlap among the three lists. If the overlapping is not present, then either you are not the person that others think you are or someone described more transient characteristics than longstanding traits.

A word about...

"What makes you, you?" Different personality theorist would answer that question differently. To some, genetics play a paramount role. That is, you inherit your traits from your parents. To others, you are nothing more than the sum of your behaviors which you learned from rewards and consequences. Others believe that unconscious motivations shape your personality. Some theorists believe that all of us are inherently good; others propose that we are essentially a "blank slate". Which of the above would you put the most faith in? That answer will, indeed, tell a lot about you.

10.2 PERSONALITY AND TEMPERAMENT

Here is an exercise which will give you some insight into the importance of temperament on your present personality. That is, it may show you that some of the characteristics with which you were born, still stay with you. Conversely, you may have learned to overcome your temperament.

GOAL: To understand the permanence of temperament

DIRECTIONS: First, take this exercise yourself on how you presently see yourself. Read each item and circle the response which you believe is most appropriate for you at this time in your life.

Second, and this may be difficult, give the questionnaire to someone (a parent, guardian, older sibling, or other close relative) who knew you as a young child.

SCORING: Finally, compare the two ratings. For most of us, there will be a high degree of similarity.

SELF TEST

For each item, circle the response as you see yourself today:

1 - Strongly Agree
2 - Agree
3 - Neutral
4 - Disagree
5 - Strongly Disagree

1.	I have a good appetite.	1	2	3	4	5
2.	I lack energy to complete tasks.	1	2	3	4	5
3.	I do not like to take risks.	1	2	3	4	5
4.	I am affectionate.	1	2	3	4	5
5.	I am fearful.	1	2	3	4	5
6.	I am jealous of others.	1	2	3	4	5
7.	I tease people.	1	2	3	4	5

1 - Strongly Agree

2 - Agree

3 - Neutral

4 - Disagree

5 - Strongly Disagree

8.	I am emotionally sensitive.	1	2	3	4	5
9.	I am fretful.	1	2	3	4	5
10.	I am enthusiastic.	1	2	3	4	5
11.	I am shy around others.	1	2	3	4	5
12.	I am mischievous.	1	2	3	4	5
13.	I "feel" for others.	1	2	3	4	5
14.	I like to win.	1	2	3	4	5
15.	I am unpredictable.	1	2	3	4	5
16.	I am neat about my appearance.	1	2	3	4	5
17.	I like to talk.	1	2	3	4	5
18.	I am polite.	1	2	3	4	5
19.	I am assertive.	1	2	3	4	5
20.	I am driven to complete tasks.	1	2	3	4	5

Name of Individual:______________________________

(To be given to someone who knew the above named person as a very young child.)

Please complete this brief inventory on the person named above **as you remember that person as a very young child.** Rate each item according to the scale below by circling the appropriate number:

1 - Strongly Agree
2 - Agree
3 - Neutral
4 - Disagree
5 - Strongly Disagree

1.	__________had a good appetite.	1	2	3	4	5
2.	__________lacked energy.	1	2	3	4	5
3.	__________was not a risk taker.	1	2	3	4	5
4.	__________was affectionate.	1	2	3	4	5
5.	__________was fearful.	1	2	3	4	5
6.	__________was jealous of others.	1	2	3	4	5
7.	__________teased people.	1	2	3	4	5
8.	__________was emotionally sensitive.	1	2	3	4	5
9.	__________was fretful.	1	2	3	4	5
10.	__________was enthusiastic.	1	2	3	4	5
11.	__________was shy around others.	1	2	3	4	5
12.	__________was mischievous.	1	2	3	4	5
13.	__________"felt" for others.	1	2	3	4	5
14.	__________liked to win.	1	2	3	4	5
15.	__________was unpredictable.	1	2	3	4	5
16.	__________was neat about appearances.	1	2	3	4	5
17.	__________was talkative.	1	2	3	4	5
18.	__________was polite.	1	2	3	4	5
19.	__________was assertive.	1	2	3	4	5
20.	__________was driven to complete tasks.	1	2	3	4	5

Did You Know That...

It may surprise you to learn that babies may be born with certain personality characteristics like sociability or shyness; boldness or caution; fearlessness or timidity. Sometimes, even identical twins have different temperaments. One pair of researchers in a 25 year longitudinal study have identified three distinct personality temperaments in children as young as two or three months. "Easy" children had little or no difficulty with normal body functions, eating, sleeping, etc. Their emotional reactions were mild in intensity and generally positive. "Slow to warm up" children had lower levels of physical activity and had some difficulty adapting to new situations. The "difficult" children had characteristics just the opposite of the "easy" children, including intense and negative emotions. Frequently, these temperamental attributes persist in to adulthood. People can change; however, changes in temperament are difficult.

10.3 AGGRESSION? SAYS WHO?

Psychologists have suggested a variety of definitions of aggression, for example, a response that delivers noxious stimuli to another organism; a response having for its goal the injury of a living organism; and behavior that results in personal injury and/or destruction of property (the injury may be psychological as well as physical). But the definitions do not always agree on what constitutes an aggressive behavior.

GOAL: To stimulate you to examine your own definition of aggression more closely.

DIRECTIONS: Listed below are a number of different actions that a person might engage in. Rate each act according to your opinion of its degree of aggressiveness. Circle the appropriate rating. (More directions will follow.)

PERSONAL RATING OF AGGRESSION

ACTION		RATING Highly Aggressive				Not at All Aggressive
1.	A baseball pitcher strikes a batter during a game.	5	4	3	2	1
2.	A man slaps his wife during an argument.	5	4	3	2	1
3.	A soldier shoots an enemy soldier during an attack in wartime.	5	4	3	2	1
4.	A mother slaps a child who misbehaves.	5	4	3	2	1
5.	A teacher disciplines a student who did not do his homework.	5	4	3	2	1
6.	A woman kills her rapist.	5	4	3	2	1
7.	A group of revolutionaries sets off a bomb at night in a bank as part of a political protest.	5	4	3	2	1
8.	A disenchanted citizen decides not to vote.	5	4	3	2	1

ACTION	Highly Aggressive				Not at All Aggressive
9. Two young children fantasize about the horrible ways in which they will get back at their enemies.	5	4	3	2	1
10. A prison warden executes a convicted criminal.	5	4	3	2	1
11. During an argument, a woman slaps her husband.	5	4	3	2	1
12. While watching a particularly bloody scene on television, a child bursts out laughing.	5	4	3	2	1
13. A person draws graffiti on the walls of a bathroom.	5	4	3	2	1
14. A person accidentally knocks a flowerpot off a ledge, which hits and injures a pedestrian.	5	4	3	2	1
15. Two people in a bar get upset and start yelling at each other.	5	4	3	2	1
16. Two police officers restrain and handcuff a demonstrator.	5	4	3	2	1

SCORING:

There is no absolute way to score what is and isn't aggressive per se, it's a matter of judgement. So, now ask another person to rate the same set of behaviors on the rating sheet below. Try to select someone whose attitudes or political philosophy is different from your own. Compare your ratings with that person's and with the ratings of other people in your class to see how and how much you differ and what is and isn't aggressive behavior.

Did You Know That...

Most people's behavior can accurately be placed on a continuum which ranges from passivity to assertiveness to aggression to hostility. Passive individuals, who were possibly born with this as a temperamental characteristic, tend to let others do as they please to them. Assertive people express their displeasure in socially appropriate ways, and yet they get their point across. Aggression results, sometimes, from frustration, especially after assertiveness failed. Hostility is rarely productive.

PERSONAL RATING OF AGGRESSION

ACTION		RATING				
	Circle your response to each action.	Highly Aggressive				Not at All Aggressive
1.	A baseball pitcher strikes a batter during a game.	5	4	3	2	1
2.	A man slaps his wife during an argument.	5	4	3	2	1
3.	A soldier shoots an enemy soldier during an attack in wartime.	5	4	3	2	1
4.	A mother slaps a child who misbehaves.	5	4	3	2	1
5.	A teacher disciplines a student who did not do his homework.	5	4	3	2	1
6.	A woman kills her rapist.	5	4	3	2	1
7.	A group of revolutionaries sets off a bomb at night in a bank as part of a political protest.	5	4	3	2	1
8.	A disenchanted citizen decides not to vote.	5	4	3	2	1
9.	Two young children fantasize about the horrible ways in which they will get back at their enemies.	5	4	3	2	1
10.	A prison warden executes a convicted criminal.	5	4	3	2	1
11.	During an argument, a woman slaps her husband.	5	4	3	2	1
12.	While watching a particularly bloody scene on television, a child bursts out laughing.	5	4	3	2	1
13.	A person draws graffiti on the walls of a bathroom.	5	4	3	2	1
14.	A person accidentally knocks a flowerpot off a ledge, which hits and injures a pedestrian.	5	4	3	2	1
15.	Two people in a bar get upset and start yelling at each other.	5	4	3	2	1
16.	Two police officers restrain and handcuff a demonstrator.	5	4	3	2	1

Do your ratings of aggressiveness agree or disagree with the ratings of the person selected to fill out the second rating sheet?

If there is disagreement, for what rated behaviors does it occur?

What is the reason for the disagreement? That is, how does your basic definition of aggression seem to differ from the other person's?

Final direction. Rate the same actions according to each of the three definitions of aggression by circling either "yes" or "no" depending on whether you think the action fits the definition.

RATING OF AGGRESSION BY DEFINITION

ACTION	DEFINITION 1: "A response that delivers noxious stimuli to another organism."		DEFINITION 2: "A response having for its goal the injury of a living organism."		DEFINITION 3: "Behavior that results in personal injury and/or destruction of property; the injury may be psychological as well as physical."	
1. A baseball pitcher strikes a batter during a game.	yes	no	yes	no	yes	no
2. A man slaps his wife during an argument.	yes	no	yes	no	yes	no
3. A soldier shoots an enemy soldier during wartime.	yes	no	yes	no	yes	no
4. A mother slaps a child who misbehaved.	yes	no	yes	no	yes	no
5. A teacher disciplines a student who did not do his homework	yes	no	yes	no	yes	no
6. A woman kills her rapist	yes	no	yes	no	yes	no

		DEFINITION 1: "A response that delivers noxious stimuli to another organism."		DEFINITION 2: "A response having for its goal the injury of a living organism."		DEFINITION 3: "Behavior that results in personal injury and/or destruction of property; the injury may be psychological as well as physical."	
7.	A group of revolutionaries sets off a bomb at night in a bank as part of a political protest.	yes	no	yes	no	yes	no
8.	A disenchanted citizen decides not to vote.	yes	no	yes	no	yes	no
9.	Two young children fantasize about the way in which they will get back at their enemies.	yes	no	yes	no	yes	no
10.	A prison warden executes a convicted criminal.	yes	no	yes	no	yes	no
11.	During an argument, a woman slaps her husband.	yes	no	yes	no	yes	no
12.	While watching a particularly bloody scene on television, a child bursts out laughing.	yes	no	yes	no	yes	no
13.	A person draws graffiti on the walls of a bathroom.	yes	no	yes	no	yes	no

		DEFINITION 1: "A response that delivers noxious stimuli to another organism."		DEFINITION 2: "A response having for its goal the injury of a living organism."		DEFINITION 3: "Behavior that results in personal injury and/or destruction of property; the injury may be psychological as well as physical."	
14.	A person accidentally knocks a flower pot off a ledge, which hits hits and injures a pedestrian.	yes	no	yes	no	yes	no
15.	Two people in a bar get upset and start yelling at each other.	yes	no	yes	no	yes	no
16.	Two police officers restrain and handcuff a demonstrator.	yes	no	yes	no	yes	no

It all depends on how we look at things, and not on how they are.
Carl Jung

It is easier to fight for one's principles than to live up to them.
Alfred Adler

If the only tool you have is a hammer,
you tend to see every problem as a nail.
Abraham Maslow

10.4 THE PERSONALITY MATCH GAME

Earlier in this book, you were asked to match a well known psychologist with the term which that psychologist would use to describe a well functioning, normal person. This exercise will ask you to match a personality theorist with key components of her/his theory.

GOAL: To connect a personality theorist with her/his theory of personality.

DIRECTIONS: Match the theorist on the left with what the theory is noted for on the right.

Theorist	Theory
1. Gordon Allport	A. Anatomy is destiny; ego personality
2. Raymond Cattell	B. Applied learning theories to Freudian concepts
3. John Dollard/Neal Miller	C. Believes that anxiety occurs when freedom is threatened.
4. Erik Erikson	D. Founder of what is now known as radical behaviorism
5. Hans Eysenck	E. Personal constructs give meaning to experience
6. Karen Horney	F. Personality dimensions of introversion/extroversion and neuroticism/psychoticism
7. George Kelly	G. Social learning theorist who looks at the person in a given situation
8. Rollo May	H. Trait theorist who emphasized importance of studying the individual
9. Walter Mischel	I. Two basic needs of infants are safety and satisfaction
10. John Watson	J. Used factor analysis to study personality

Correct Answers:

1. Allport	H
2. Cattell	J
3. Dollard/Miller	B
4. Erikson	A
5. Eysenck	F
6. Horney	I
7. Kelly	E
8. May	C
9. Mischel	G
10. Watson	D

SCORING:

If you scored 8 - 10 correctly, you have a solid knowledge of personality theorist (and, who knows, it may help you at a party.)

If you scored 5 - 7 correctly, your knowledge level is adequate and you still have a life outside of class.

If you scored fewer than 5 correctly, perhaps you see things differently from others and you may be able to develop your own theory to explain why people behave the way that they do.

11

SECTION ELEVEN: PSYCHOLOGICAL DISORDERS

To say that there is such a thing as normal implies that there must also be abnormal. There is, however, no simple way to distinguish between the two. Rather than being black and white opposites, the states lie on a continuum. The business and economics majors in group will perhaps see the irony of a section 11 dealing with psychological disorders. (For the uninitiated, this is how companies file for protection under bankruptcy laws.) Of course, there are non economic reasons for maladaptive thoughts and behaviors that cause the persons who hold them considerable distress. The tasks in this section look at some of them.

The first item is again one which we use with our classes. Simply put, you are asked to convince yourself that you are normal. (Fortunately, no one turned the tables on us and asked us this question.) The next set of questions looks at eating disorders. Then, you are asked to determine your reaction to some commonly feared items. The fourth exercise is a cognitive-behavioral assessment of fears. And finally, on the lighter side, we ask you to identify phobias when given some unusual clues.

Two notes. First there is a tendency to take a physical or psychological disorder checklist and come away convinced that you suffer from whatever malady you have just been asked about. Second, you may need to consult with an old-timer, (at least 35 years old) to help you with some of the clues in the fifth exercise. If you are going to share this one with your friends you may want to have fun and create your own clues.

We realize that psychological disorders are serious. We hoped that we presented the material in a way which gets this message to you while simultaneously holding your interest. (Come to think of it, that is the goal of this entire book!)

Psychological Disorders exercises include:

11.1 ARE YOU NORMAL?

Most of us take normality for granted. However, some people believe that there is no such thing as abnormal. To look at this problem, we developed this exercise.

GOAL: To help you see what normal is.

DIRECTIONS: Write a one page essay on what you do that convinces you that you are normal. (Hint: average as in height, weight, blood pressure, does not equate to normality.) After you have written your paper, turn to the next page to see if your ideas contained some of the concepts which typify normality.

SCORING:

While there is no single right or wrong answer to this, the list below contains some of the most common traits that are considered normal in our society. The more of these kinds of traits you have, the closer to the norm you are.

1. Commitment to goals.
2. Commitment to family.
3. Ability to share.
4. Ability to have positive relationships with others.
5. Commitment to self preservation (do not abuse your body).
6. Affiliations/belongingness.
7. Willingness to sacrifice.
8. Ability to have fun.
9. Moderation and balance in activities.
10. Spirituality; morality, ethics.
11. Diversity of interests.
12. Ability to learn from mistakes.
13. Respect for life.
14. Productive use of time (work, school, etc.).
15. Respect for what is not yours (environment, property).

11.2 COULD YOU BECOME ANOREXIC OR BULIMIC ?

One in every 200 teenage girls in America starves herself. Nearly 1 in every 4 binges and purges. Eight percent of anorexics and bulimics will die. Now, most of us have relatively healthy, stable eating habits. But-even if you don't have either of these disorders now, there are signs that'll show you whether your attitude toward food makes you a likely candidate. Answer the following questions and find out.

GOAL: To help identify your possible risk of becoming anorexic or bulimic

DIRECTIONS: Read each item and circle "YES" or "NO" as appropriate.

1.	Do you usually feel uncomfortable eating in front of other people?	YES	NO
2.	Do you generally make a point of eating less than the people around you?	YES	NO
3.	Do you usually stop eating before you are full?	YES	NO
4.	When you are depressed, nervous or under stress, do you overeat to make yourself feel better?	YES	NO
5.	Do you talk a lot about what and how much you eat?	YES	NO
6.	Are you always looking for the "perfect" diet?	YES	NO
7.	Do you frequently skip meals just so you won't gain weight?	YES	NO
8.	Do you ever feel so guilty about eating something that you don't finish it?	YES	NO
9.	Have you ever forced yourself to vomit after a meal?	YES	NO
10.	Have you ever lied about "not feeling hungry" just to get out of eating a meal?	YES	NO
11.	Do you choose foods based on how many calories they have? (For example, would you choose a diet soda over a regular one, even though you prefer the taste of a regular one?)	YES	NO
12.	Have you ever taken laxatives or diuretics in order to lose weight quickly?	YES	NO
13.	Do you reward yourself when you accomplish something by eating "forbidden foods" - things you've otherwise eliminated from your diet?	YES	NO
14.	Do you feel like you've failed if you eat the "wrong" foods or break your diet?	YES	NO
15.	Do you only feel good about yourself as a person when you are losing weight?	YES	NO

SCORING:

Now tally up all the times you answered yes to get your score.

1-6: Most of us do some of these things some of the time. It's nothing to get worried about. Just be sure that your eating patterns don't get out of control and become destructive to your health or your happiness. Remember that doggy old line about you are what you eat? Well, as far as your health is concerned, it's true.

7-11: We'll never tell you to base your diet on what other people eat, but the next time you and your friends sit down for lunch, pay attention to what and how much they eat-just so you can get some perspective on what and how much *you're* really eating. For example, if you're eating less than half of what friends your age and size eat, then you're probably not eating enough. And remember, the good old four food groups are vital, and your body needs about 1,000 calories daily just to function (meaning breathe and walk) day after day.

12-15: If you scored in this category, you should take a good look at your eating habits. It sounds like they're on the verge of becoming destructive and now's the time to get them under control again. Talk to a level-headed friend who will be honest with you about how you look, your weight and the things you do-and don't-eat. It would be a good idea to see a doctor too, just for a checkup, to make sure you're healthy. If you're not, and he or she feels that it's a result of your eating habits, you may be referred to a specialist-like a nutritionist or a psychologist. The thing to remember here is that there is nothing to be ashamed or scared of unless you ignore the problem. It's true that no one can force you to eat right. That's up to you. So do it for yourself.

For More Information On... anorexia and/or bulimia, contact:

Eating Disorders Awareness and Prevention, Inc. (EDAP)
603 Stewart Street, Suite 803
Seattle, WA 98101
206-382-3587

American Anorexia/Bulimia Association, Inc.
293 Central Park West
New York, NY 10024
212-501-8351

National Association of Anorexia Nervosa and Associated Disorders
Box 7
Highland park, IL 600355
708-433-4632

11.3 ARE YOU AFRAID OF... ?

The Temple Fear Survey

Are you bothered by things such as loud noises, cars, being alone, taking tests etc. What objects or events make you cringe? Take the Temple Fear Survey and then compare your score with a sample from Temple University.

GOAL: To ascertain the types of things which you fear and to compare your fears with the fears of students at Temple University.

DIRECTIONS: How much do each of the items listed bother you? Write a number from one to five, according to the scale below, next to each item listed.

1 - None 2 - Some 3 - Much 4 - Very Much 5 - Terror!

___ 1. Noise of vacuum cleaners
___ 2. Being cut
___ 3. Being alone
___ 4. Speaking before a group
___ 5. Dead bodies
___ 6. Loud noises
___ 7. Being a passenger in a car
___ 8. Driving a car
___ 9. Auto accidents
___10. People with deformities
___11. Being in a strange place
___12. Riding a roller coaster
___13. Being in closed places
___14. Thunder
___15. Falling down
___16. One person bullying another
___17. Being bullied by someone
___18. Loud sirens
___19. Doctors
___20. High places
___21. Being teased
___22. Dentists
___23. Cemeteries
___24. Strangers
___25. Being physically assaulted
___26. Failing a test
___27. Not being a success
___28. Losing a job
___29. Making a mistake
___30. Sharp objects (Knives, razors....)
___31. Death
___32. Death of a loved one
___33. Worms
___34. Imaginary creatures
___35. Dark places
___36. Strange dogs
___37. Receiving injections
___38. Seeing other people injected
___39. Illness
___40. Angry people
___41. Mice and rats
___42. Fire

SOURCE: Reprinted with the permission from *Behavior Research and Therapy, 7,* (1969) "A Factor Analysis of a 100 item Fear Survey Inventory", pages 399-402 by P.R. Braun & D J. Reynolds. Elsevier Science Ltd., Pergamon Imprint, Oxford, England.

1 - None 2 - Some 3 - Much 4 - Very Much 5 - Terror!

___43. Ugly people
___44. Snakes
___45. Lightning
___46. Sudden noises
___47. Swimming alone

___48. Witnessing a surgical operation
___49. Prospects of a surgical operation
___50. Deep water
___51. Dead animals
___52. Blood
___53. Seeing a fight
___54. Being in a fight
___55. Being criticized
___56. Suffocating
___57. Looking foolish
___58. Being a passenger in an airplane
___59. Arguing with parents
___60. Meeting someone for the first time
___61. Being misunderstood
___62. Crowded places
___63. Being a leader
___64. Losing control
___65. Being with drunks
___66. Being self-conscious
___67. People in authority
___68. People who seem insane
___69. Boating
___70. God
___72. Stinging insects
___73. Crawling insects
___74. Flying insects
___75. Crossing streets
___76. Entering a room where other people are seated
___ 77. Bats
___ 78. Journeys by train
___ 79. Journeys by bus
___ 80. Feeling angry
___ 81. Dull weather
___ 82. Large open spaces
___ 83. Cuts
___ 84. Tough-looking people
___ 85. Birds
___ 86. Being watched while working
___ 87. Guns
___ 88. Dirt
___ 89. Being in an elevator
___ 90. Parting from friends
___ 91. Feeling rejected by others
___ 92. Odors
___ 93. Feeling disapproved of
___ 94. Being ignored
___ 95. Premature heart beats
___ 96. Nude men
___ 97. Nude women
___ 98. Unclean silverware in restaurants
___ 99. Dirty restrooms
___100. Becoming mentally ill

SCORING:

Now that you have completed the survey yourself, you can compare your answers to those of a sample of 435 introductory psychology students at Temple University by referring to the following table which shows the mean or average score for each question for males and females.

MEAN	SCORE		MEAN	SCORE		MEAN	SCORE	
	Male	Female		Male	Female		Male	Female
1.	1.1	1.0	35.	1.5	2.0	68.	2.1	2.3
2.	2.2	2.2	36.	1.8	2.0	69.	1.3	1.5
3.	1.5	1.7	37.	1.8	1.9	70.	1.6	1.5
4.	2.4	2.6	38.	1.5	1.7	71.	1.4	2.1
5.	2.0	2.8	39.	1.8	1.9	72.	2.0	2.4
6.	1.5	1.7	40.	1.7	1.9	73.	1.7	2.3
7.	1.3	1.2	41.	1.6	2.6	74.	1.6	2.1
8.	1.2	1.5	42.	1.8	2.7	75.	1.1	1.1
9.	2.5	2.9	43.	1.3	1.3	76.	1.6	1.7
10.	1.5	1.6	44.	2.0	2.8	77.	1.9	2.7
11.	1.6	1.8	45.	1.4	1.9	78.	1.1	1.1
12.	2.0	2.1	46	1.8	2.1	79.	1.1	1.1
13.	1.5	1.6	47.	1.6	1.8	80.	1.4	1.4
14.	1.1	1.5	48.	1.9	1.7	81.	1.1	1.1
15.	1.6	1.8	49.	2.5	2.7	82.	1.1	1.1
16.	1.7	1.8	50.	1.7	2.1	83.	1.7	1.8
17.	2.0	2.0	51.	1.4	2.0	84.	1.7	2.0
18.	1.3	1.7	52.	1.6	1.8	85.	1.1	1.2
19.	1.5	1.6	53.	1.5	1.9	86.	1.8	1.9
20.	2.0	2.1	54.	2.2	2.6	87.	1.6	2.2
21.	1.6	1.6	55.	2.0	2.1	88.	1.1	1.2
22.	1.9	2.1	56.	2.5	2.6	89.	1.1	1.4
23.	1.4	1.6	57.	2.3	2.3	90.	1.7	1.9
24.	1.4	1.6	58.	1.5	1.7	91.	2.2	2.4
25.	2.2	3.1	59.	1.6	1.6	92.	1.4	1.3
26.	2.6	2.7	60.	1.6	1.7	93.	2.3	2.3
27.	2.7	2.4	61.	1.7	1.9	94.	2.0	2.1
28.	2.1	2.0	62.	1.4	1.4	95.	1.6	1.5
29.	2.2	2.1	63.	1.5	1.7	96.	1.1	1.7
30.	1.7	1.7	64.	1.7	1.7	97.	1.1	1.2
31.	2.4	2.7	65.	1.7	2.2	98.	1.8	1.9
32.	3.0	3.4	66.	1.9	2.1	99.	1.9	2.1
33.	1.2	1.8	67.	1.4	1.5	100.	2.1	2.0
34.	1.2	1.4						

How did your scores compare with the group from Temple University? Some items provoked relatively high levels of fear such as "death of a loved one" (item 32), "failing a test" (item 26), and "suffocating" (item 56). Did the results surprise you? If so, which ones and in which direction (more or less fearful)?

Thinking is like living and dying. Each of us must do it for himself.
Josiah Royce

Razors pain you
Rivers are damp;
Acids stain you;
And drugs cause cramp.
Guns aren't lawful;
Nooses give;
Gas smells awful;
You might as well live.
Dorothy Parker

11.4 DO YOUR OWN THOUGHTS PUT YOU: DOWN IN THE DUMPS?

Cognitive theorists believe that **the way we evaluate** a given event (being stuck in traffic, having to make a presentation before a group, etc.) is **more critical than the event itself**. That is, if we view a traffic jam as an opportunity to delay the arrival of an aversive occurrence (like getting to work), then the emotional reaction on our part would be relief. Conversely, if we view the same event (the traffic jam) as the cause of losing a job, then the reaction would be one of anger or depression. To cognitive theorists, as initially expressed by the first century philosopher Epictetus, maladaptive responses are caused not by the event itself, but rather by the view we take of it. In a sense, we do indeed drive ourselves crazy with our own thoughts!

The list which follows contains the type of thoughts which can be linked to depression. See how many of these permeate your thoughts and perhaps "put you down in the dumps."

GOAL: To demonstrate how thoughts and internal verbalizations can lead to maladaptive emotional and/or behavioral consequences.

DIRECTIONS: Using the code below, indicate how frequently you have the following thoughts in response to "everyday" occurrences. However, after you have completed the list, try to come up with other less draconian thoughts which may merely sadden, but not depress, you.

1 - Never 2 - Seldom 3 - Often 4 - Very Often

__ 1. It seems such an effort to do anything.
__ 2. I feel pessimistic about the future.
__ 3. I have too many bad things in my life.
__ 4. I have little to look forward to.
__ 5. I'm drained of energy, worn out.
__ 6. I'm not as successful as other people.
__ 7. Everything seems futile and pointless.
__ 8. I just want to curl up and go to sleep.
__ 9. There are things about me that I don't like.
__10. It's too much effort even to move.
__11. I'm absolutely exhausted.
__12. The future seems just one string of problems.
__13. My thoughts keep drifting away.

1 - Never 2 - Seldom 3 - Often 4 - Very Often

__14. I get no satisfaction from the things I do.
__15. I've made so many mistakes in the past.
__16. I've got to really concentrate just to keep my eyes open.
__17. Everything I do turns out badly.
__18. My whole body has slowed down.
__19. I regret some of the things I've done.
__20. I can't make the effort to liven up myself.
__21. I feel depressed with the way things are going.
__22. I haven't any real friends anymore.
__23. I do have a number of problems.
__24. There's no one I can feel really close to.
__25. I wish I were someone else.
__26. I'm annoyed at myself for being bad at making decisions.
__27. I don't make a good impression on other people.
__28. The future looks hopeless.
__29. I don't get the same satisfaction out of things these days.
__30. I wish something would happen to make me feel better.

SCORING: (By Donovan & Rosato)

30 - 45 points: It is unlikely that you "awfulize" events. Your philosophical outlook seems to be positive.

46 - 60 points: Your thoughts and beliefs rarely lead to anxiety and depression. Keep up the good thoughts.

61 - 90 points: There is some degree of likelihood that your belief system may cause you psychological distress. Try to look at events less catastrophically.

91 - 120 points: One may reasonably conclude that people who accumulate this many points on this exercise **NEED TO LIGHTEN UP!**

A Word About...

cognitive therapy for depression. As stated in our introduction to this exercise, cognitive therapists put great emphasis of the way people "evaluate" ideas and beliefs. These therapists believe that depressed individuals attribute any success to "luck" and any failure to inherent weaknesses. Therapy consists of trying to help the person have a more balanced and accurate view of life. A technique used is called disputing. The therapist has the client/patient "prove" that there are "too many bad things in my life" (item 3). The client/ patient is actually taught to "argue" with herself/himself.

11.5 DO FEARS PUT YOU IN JEOPARDY?

First of all, we realize that phobias are no laughing matter. Unrealistic (in the eyes of **others**) fears do produce anxious reactions. However, we believe that a good way to help to identify some common (and a few less common) phobias is by following the format of a popular television game.

GOAL: To help identify phobias by their name.

DIRECTIONS: You will be given the name of a response . Your job is to provide the appropriate question which includes a phobia. For example, the answer is "People with this have no problem coming out of the closet". Your question should be " what is claustrophobia"? Check yourself on the next page.

See, there is nothing to be afraid of with this exercise.

ANSWERS:

1. Erika Jong piloted this idea and probably didn't know it.
2. People with this should not apply for jobs as elevator operators at the World Trade Center.
3. Don't tell Forest Gump about this.
4. Keep the mosquitos away from these people.
5. Garfield probably feels the same way about them. They should also avoid a certain play.
6. Keep Madonna away from these people.
7. Margaret Mead would be in trouble if she felt this way.
8. You'd be in trouble if your lifeguard had this.
9. Willard Scott would be sympathetic.
10. If Indiana Jones had this, he'd be in big trouble.
11. Too many "Jason movies" could lead to this.
12. I'm not sure that Robert James Waller had this mind when he wrote his book.
13. Pigpen (from Peanuts) probably does not have this.
14. This is a transient condition at term paper and exam time.
15. People with this might have a difficult time on New York City Subways.
16. These people should not move to Montana.
17. *Charlotte's Web* is probably not their favorite book.
18. James Heriot does not have this.
19. When Santa Claus comes to town, these people leave.
20. A film developer would not be successful with this condition.

Now look at the phobias to see how you did.

1. What is *aviophobia* (fear of flying)?
2. What is *acrophobia* (fear of heights)?
3. What is *dromophobia* (fear of running)?
4. What is *acarophobia* (fear of itching)?
5. What is *ailurophobia* (fear of cats)?
6. What is *erythrophobia* (fear of blushing)?
7. What is *anthrophobia* (fear of human society)?
8. What is *aquaphobia* (fear of water)?
9. What is *astraphobia* (fear of thunder, storms, and lightning)?
10. What is *ophidiophobia* (fear of snakes)?
11. What is *triskaidekaphobia* (fear of number 13)?
12. What is *gephydrophobia* (fear of bridges)?
13. What is *mysophobia* (fear of dirt and germs)?
14. What is *graphophobia* (fear of writing)?
15. What is *xenophobia* (fear of strangers)?
16. What is *agoraphobia* (fear of open spaces)?
17. What is *arachnophobia* (fear of spiders)?
18. What is *zoophobia* (fear of animals)?
19. What is *phgonophobia* (fear of beards)?
20. What is *nyctophobia* (fear of dark)?

Admittedly, these are difficult and some of the hints were obscure. So, **fear not** if you did not get all of them right. Anything more than half should be considered a success. And please, do not develop *falleraphobia* (fear of failing)!

Did You Know That...

A common method of treating phobias is through systematic desensitization. The therapist induces a level of relaxation in the client/patient by asking the person to imagine a particularly calming scene (like lying on a beach). The therapist then gradually introduces topics related to the phobic item. Once the client/patient begins to experience even the slightest apprehension, the therapist instructs the client/ patient to think back to the relaxation scene. The idea is to pair a sense of relaxation with the previously feared item. The theory is that since fear and relaxation cannot co-exist in the individual at the same time, the person will learn to associate the feared object with a sense of calmness. Of course, full recovery frequently requires a successful encounter with the feared object.

12

SECTION TWELVE: TREATMENT AND THERAPY

In the previous section, we spoke to you about various psychological maladies which afflict as many as 10 percent of all adults at any given time. The exercises in this section will, hopefully, give you some insight into the many procedures that exist for treating such conditions. Our goal is to provide you with some therapy techniques which you might find helpful.

The first exercise is Practicing Assertive Communication. The intent of this task is to give you the opportunity to respond appropriately to a number of potentially frustrating and/or sticky situations. As you might have gathered from the previous section, an inappropriate reaction to some of these situations could lead to maladaptive emotions or behaviors. We hope to teach some preventive techniques with this exercise.

The second set of items are also in the self-help domain. We want to show you ways to change some unwanted behaviors. The third exercise is one of our own. Once again, we resort back to the tried and true method of matching to assess your knowledge of various treatment approaches. Finally, we want you to gain some insight into the factors which go into deciding whether or not to seek professional help. If nothing else, you'll gain some empathy for those who face such decisions.

As we said in Section 9, you will not be able to open your own treatment facility at the end of this section. However, you should know some beneficial ways to prevent psychological problems and be able to make some changes in the way you behave. You'll also have a clearer understanding of the theory of treatment. All of this, and you did not have to buy another self help book!

Treatment exercises include:

12.1 Practicing Assertive Communication
12.2 Using Modeling Principles In Your Daily Life
12.3 Different Strokes
12.4 Attitudes Toward Seeking Professional Help

12.1 PRACTICING ASSERTIVE COMMUNICATION

Each day we find ourselves attempting to deal with conflicts with others. Many of us often wish we had handled these conflicts differently, as is evidenced by the frequency of such statements as, "I wish I had said this . . . ." or "I wish I had another chance to . . . ." Becoming assertive takes practice. Sometimes we need to rehearse our assertive communication ahead of time so that when situations arise that call for assertiveness, we are prepared. We have included our own (D & R) example to help get you started.

GOAL: To develop skills in assertive communication

DIRECTIONS: Practice writing several assertive statements for each of the following situations.

Example: You have dated someone once or twice and are not interested in seeing this person again. But, the other person seems interested in you. You will be seeing this person at a social function later tonight. What will you say if he or she asks you when you will be getting together again?

Nonassertive response: *I've had a lot going on. I have a really busy semester and just don't have time for much of a social life. Maybe I'll see you when I can take a break.*

Problem: You never clearly express your desire to stop seeing this person. You allow the other person to infer that you have a future together when you use the words "maybe" and "this semester" as if this is only a temporary problem. You also box yourself in by saying you have no social life yet here you are at a social function! Worst of all, you blame your failure on making a date on an external circumstance--a busy semester--instead of a stable, internal condition: your own desire not to continue the dating relationship.

Assertive response: *I have enjoyed our time together but I'm not interested in pursuing a dating relationship with you. I don't feel comfortable discussing all my feelings, and I like you so I don't want to hurt your feelings, either. I hope we can still be friends, because I will be glad to see you when we do run into each other.*

Advantages: You have told the truth, so you don't have to remember what you said or make up a new story every time you run into this person. You have not been defensive or tried to "explain" your feelings. You have expressed a desire to be kind and friendly to the other person. Now the ball is in his or her court about whether to continue as friends--or not. Either way, you have been truthful, kind, and clear.

The rest of the exercises are up to you.

SOURCE: Reprinted by permission from page 328 of *Adjustment and Growth in a Changing World* 3/e by Napoli, Kilbride, &Tebbs;

1. You are in a restaurant and have ordered a steak, medium rare. When the steak arrives you discover that it is very rare. The waiter leaves and does not return for quite some time. Finally the waiter arrives and asks if you are enjoying your meal? You respond,

____

____

____

2. You have been working for a company for one month. Because you have wanted to be accepted and liked by your new boss, you have worked overtime on several occasions. You have made plans to go out with a friend immediately after work today. Just as it is time to leave, your boss asks you if you will stay and work two more hours. You respond,

____

____

____

3. Your doctor prescribes medication for a current ailment. When you ask him what you have, he responds by telling you not to worry because it is nothing major. You respond,

____

____

____

4. A salesperson approaches you and asks if she can be of assistance. You respond, "No thank you. I am just looking right now." The salesperson continues to follow you as you walk, telling you that you would look nice in nearly everything you see. You begin to be annoyed and respond by saying,

____

____

____

5. You are the parent of three children from age five to eleven. One day you discover that you are yelling at them because they do not seem to be listening to you. The more you yell, the less they seem to listen. Deciding on another approach, you say to them,

____

____

____

6. You have been married to your mate for nearly eight years. In the beginning of your relationship, sex with each other was more frequent. The last time you attempted to discuss the infrequency of sex with your mate, he/she got angry and refused to talk about it. Realizing that the problem is continuing, you decide to make an attempt at open communication again. You say,

____

____

____

7. Your grandmother, whom you have not talked to in six months, calls you on the telephone just as you are in the middle of discussing the recent infrequency of sex with your mate. You say,

____

____

____

8. A friend invites you to a large party so you can meet some "influential people." When you arrive, everyone seems to be in small groups or paired off with someone. You begin to feel lonely and uncomfortable. As you gaze around the room, you notice a person of the opposite sex standing by the punch bowl. You walk up and say,

____

____

____

SCORING:

There are no right or wrong answers per se. The goal is to practice communicating what you think and feel in a clear and direct manner, that is to say assertively, without going to either extreme of holding in your feelings (by being passive) or getting pushy and/or losing your temper over not getting what you want (being aggressive). Discuss your statements with other classmates and encourage them to discuss their statements with you. You can learn from each other.

12.2 USING MODELING PRINCIPLES IN YOUR DAILY LIFE

This exercise is designed to help you identify behaviors you might want to learn or modify using a model. It is particularly helpful for skill-related concerns.

GOAL: To help you to change some unwanted behaviors.

DIRECTIONS: Follow the instructions below. An example using the responses of a student is included for each part.

Think of a skill or ability that you want to learn or modify. Develop a list of 2 to 3 skills. Try to list only those skills that you believe observing and imitating someone else might help you to acquire. *Example*: Play golf, drive a car, learn to cook oriental foods, learn to interview for a job, play the guitar better, write a term paper.

Select one of the skills you identified above that you want to work on during the next few weeks. Try to be as specific as possible about the aspects of that skill you want to learn. *Example*: Play the guitar better. I want to learn how to play a rhythm pattern to a rock and roll song entitled, "It's so Easy to Fall in Love."

List several people who could act as models for you to learn that skill. Example: Jack, a friend who has been playing guitar a bit longer than I have; Sally, a friend who plays professionally with a group; Joan, a classmate who studies stringed instruments in the College Conservatory of Music.

Select one of those people. To aid your selection process, use the behaviors and other characteristics of good models who you know. Try to select someone from your list that you think would best meet these characteristics, or who is likely to want to engage in some of the behaviors described. *Example*: I think I'll use Jack. I like and respect him, he is similar to me in age and interests, and he plays just a little bit better than I do. He is also not a perfect guitar player and makes a few mistakes for time to time.

What will you have to do to make the best use of the model you selected? What are some things you must do and what are some things you might want to tell your model to gain the maximum benefit from the experience? *Example*: I suppose I should tell Jack to play the song a couple of times so I can hear how good it sounds when it's played correctly. I should ask him to play each bar and I'll try to do it as he does. I'll ask him to talk about what he's doing and to guide me verbally if needed.

Try your plan for a week or two. Evaluate how well things are going and make any corrections in it that you think are needed before continuing with it beyond the initial time period.

SOURCE: Reprinted by permission from page 79 of *Adjustment and Competence: Concepts & Applications* by Grasha and Kirschenbaum;

Nobody realizes that some people expend tremendous energy merely to be normal.
Albert Camus

He who fears he will suffer, already suffers because of his fear.
Montaigne

To err is dysfunctional, to forgive, co-dependent.
Berton Averre

12.3 DIFFERENT STROKES

As you've probably gathered by this time in the course, different philosophical and theoretical orientations exist. Each orientation believes that it has "the answer". This exercise will ask you to match the 5 major theoretical therapy orientations with their explanation of the "cause" of the problem and with their approach to treatment.

GOAL: To increase your understanding of various approaches to treatment.

DIRECTIONS: Match the theoretical orientation with the cause and then with the treatment approach. Complete this exercise twice, once before completing the section and once after, comparing your pre and post scores.

ORIENTATION	*CAUSE*	*TREATMENT APPROACH*
1. Cognitive	A. Biological drives conflict with societal demands	I. Discovery of unconscious motives
2. Humanistic	B. Faulty belief system	ii. Logical disputing of ideas
3. Psychoanalytic	C. Inappropriate reinforcement	iii. Modeling
4. Strict Behaviorism	D. Lack of self-efficacy	iv. Unconditional positive regard
5. Social Learning	E. Societal demands thwart personal growth	v. Unlearning

Correct Sequence::

1-B-ii

2-E-iv

3-A-i

4-C-v

5-D-iii

SCORING:

1 point for each correctly matched cause
1 point for each correctly matched approach
1 point for each perfect match

Maximum of 15 points

14-15 points = Hall of Fame Level

11-13 points = All Star Level

8-10 points = Shows Potential

Below 8 = Needs Some Seasoning

12.4 ATTITUDES TOWARD SEEKING PROFESSIONAL PSYCHOLOGICAL HELP

One of the most important decisions confronting an individual who is suffering from emotional pain is whether or not to seek professional help from a qualified therapist. Making the initial therapy contact, of course, is usually the most difficult step in the process. There is still a stigma about emotional difficulties. Some equate emotional distress with character weakness. Indeed, the seeking of help under such circumstances adds to the person's stress level. Many conclude that it is easier to live (should we say suffer) through it than to seek help.

With that thought in mind, Psychologists Edward Fischer and John Turner developed the following scale that would assess an individual's likelihood of seeking professional help. The authors recognized the need to understand the initial reluctance. They wrote, "One person may view the decision to get professional help as a sign of personal weakness, indicative of failure; for him the move to get professional help represents a last-ditch desperate action spurred by a psychologically intolerable situation." Others, however, gladly seek help and are better off because of it.

The need for therapy is obviously a serious one for some people. The willingness with which individuals agree to seek help is a potent predictor of the therapy's success.

GOAL: To gain an understanding of the issues involved in seeking psychological help.

DIRECTIONS: On the next pages are a number of statements pertaining to seeking psychological assistance. Read each statement carefully and respond according to the scale below.

0 - Disagreement 1 - Probable Disagreement 2 - Probable Agreement 3 - Agreement

____ 1. Although there are clinics for people with mental troubles, I would not have much faith in them.
____ 2. If a good friend asked my advice about a mental health problem, I might recommend that he see a psychiatrist.
____ 3. I would feel uneasy going to a psychiatrist because of what people would think.
____ 4. A person with a strong character can get over mental conflicts by himself, and would have little need of a psychiatrist.
____ 5. There are times when I have felt completely lost and would have welcomed professional advice for a personal or emotional problem.
____ 6. Considering the time and expense involved in psychotherapy, it would have doubtful value for a person like me.
____ 7. I would willingly confide intimate matters to an appropriate person if I thought it might help me or a member of my family.

0 - Disagreement 1 - Probable Disagreement 2 - Probable Agreement 3 - Agreement

_____ 8. I would rather live with certain mental conflicts than go through the ordeal of getting psychiatric treatment.
_____ 9. Emotional difficulties, like many things, tend to work out by themselves.
_____ 10. There are certain problems that should not be discussed outside one's immediate family.
_____ 11. A person with a serious emotional disturbance would probably feel more secure in a good mental hospital.
_____ 12. If I believed I was having a mental breakdown, my first inclination would be to get professional attention.
_____ 13. Keeping one's mind on a job is a good solution for avoiding personal worries and concerns.
_____ 14. Having been a psychiatric patient is a blot on a person's life.
_____ 15. I would rather be advised by a close friend than by a psychologist, even for an emotional problem.
_____ 16. A person with an emotional problem is not likely to solve it alone; he is likely to solve it with professional help.
_____ 17. I resent a person- professionally trained or not- who wants to know about my personal difficulties.
_____ 18. I would want to get psychiatric attention if I was worried or upset for a long period of time.
_____ 19. The idea of talking about problems with a psychologist strikes me as a poor way to get rid of emotional conflicts.
_____ 20. Having been mentally ill carries with it a burden of shame.
_____ 21. There are experiences in my life that I would not discuss with anyone.
_____ 22. It is probably best not to know *everything* about oneself.
_____ 23. If I were experiencing a serious emotional crisis at this point in my life, I would be confident that I could find relief in psychotherapy.
_____ 24. There is something admirable in the attitude of a person who is willing to cope with his conflicts and fears *without* resorting to professional help.
_____ 25. At some future time I might want to have psychological counseling.
_____ 26. A person should work out his own problems; getting psychological counseling would be a last resort.
_____ 27. Had I received treatment in a mental hospital, I would not feel it had to be "covered up."
_____ 28. If I thought I needed psychiatric help, I would get it no matter who knew about it.
_____ 29. It is difficult to talk about personal affairs even with highly educated people such as doctors, teachers, and clergymen.

SCORING:

(Donovan & Rosato) Reverse your scores (a 3 becomes a 0; a 2 becomes a 1; a 1 is now a 2; and a 0 a 3) for questions 1,3,4,6,8,9,10,14,15,17,19,20,21,22,24,26,29. Now total your corrected score. The higher your score the more likely you are to seek out help when you need it. If your score is a low one, consider why you are so resistant to seeking help and what this attitude may be costing you in mental and emotional distress.

Interpretation: Below 15: You are highly likely to seek help, if needed. 16-29: You would at least consider seeking professional help, if needed. 30-44: You have real doubts about the benefits of professional help. Above 44: Stay away from therapists, for their own good!

13

SECTION THIRTEEN: SOCIAL ASPECTS OF PSYCHOLOGY

Social psychology examines how the individual functions in a social or group setting. This field of psychology includes topics in social thinking (understanding causes, thinking about people, forming attitudes and prejudices) and social behaviors (influencing each other, helping or hurting each other) and interacting socially (forming relationships, making peace).

The first set of questions seeks your opinion on your perceived (there is that word again) relationship with a designated peer group. The second exercise is designed to show the ill effects of prejudices. The next two exercises asks you first to view your class as a "group" while the other requires you to become a television news critic for a week to see if you perceive if there is a "slant" or prejudice to the news. (Social psychologists love to study prejudice even more than they love "perceived"; but perceived prejudices really makes their day.) How else could we end this section but with an exercise which asks you to rate your own prejudices? This, we think, is a fun section.

Although you will be neither a psychologist, sociologist, or social psychologist, you will understand stereotyping and the effect of prejudice a bit more. You'll also be a more informed consumer of newscasts. The value of this opus keeps growing with each section.

Social Aspects of Psychology exercises include:

13.1 Index of Peer Relations
13.2 Effects of Using Stereotypes
13.3 Class Pie
13.4 Good News and Bad News
13.5 Rate Your Prejudices

13.1 INDEX OF PEER RELATIONS

On the next page appears the Index of Peer Relations (IPR). It was created by the Walmyr Publishing Company. They are one of a number of companies that specialize in the creation and sales of various psychological instruments.

Please turn the page now and complete the exercise, when you are done, turn back to this page to score your responses. **TURN THE PAGE NOW**.

To interpret your score on the IPR, after completing the questionnaire, reverse your scores for questions 1, 4, 7, 8, 11, 12, 15, 16, 17, 18, 21, 22. That is, for those questions only a:

1 = 7
2 = 6
3 = 5
4 = 4
5 = 3
6 = 2
7 = 1

Now, using your corrected scores, calculate your total overall score. The higher your score, the worse are your relationships with your peers. The maximum score is 175, any score over 125 is cause for concern and worth seeking help with.

INDEX OF PEER RELATIONS (IPR)

Name: ______________________ Today's Date: ____________

Peer Group: ______________________

This questionnaire is designed to measure the way you feel about the people you work, play, or associate with most of the time; your peer group. It is not a test, so there are no right or wrong answers. Place the name of your peer group at the top of the page in the space provided. Then answer each item as carefully and as accurately as you can by placing a number beside each one as follows.

1 = None of the time
2 = Very rarely
3 = A little of the time
4 = Some of the time
5 = A good part of the time
6 = Most of the time
7 = All of the time

---

1. ____ I get along very well with my peers.
2. ____ My peers act like they don't care about me.
3. ____ My peers treat me badly.
4. ____ My peers really seem to respect me.
5. ____ I don't feel like am "part of the group".
6. ____ My peers are a bunch of snobs.
7. ____ My peers understand me.
8. ____ My peers seem to like me very much.
9. ____ I really feel "left out" of my peer group.
10. ____ I hate my present peer group.
11. ____ My peers seem to like having me around.
12. ____ I really like my present peer group.
13. ____ I really feel like I am disliked by my peers.
14. ____ I wish I had a different peer group.
15. ____ My peers are very nice to me.
16. ____ My peers seem to look up to me.
17. ____ My peers think I am important to them.
18. ____ My peers are a real source of pleasure to me.
19. ____ My peers don't seem to even notice me.
20. ____ I wish I were not part of this peer group.
21. ____ My peers regard my ideas and opinions very highly.
22. ____ I feel like I am an important member of my peer group.
23. ____ I can't stand to be around my peer group.
24. ____ My peers seem to look down on me.
25. ____ My peers really do not interest me.

1, 4, 7, 8, 11, 12, 15, 16, 17, 18, 21, 22.

13.2 THE EFFECTS OF USING STEREOTYPES

This activity is designed to show you how various stereotypes interfere with our ability to understand people, objects, and events in our lives. Please follow the instructions carefully.

GOAL: To demonstrate the effects of stereotyping on behavior

DIRECTIONS: Sit back and relax. Think about a peanut in its shell. If a man from Mars asked you to describe the peanut so he would be able to know what a peanut was like, what would you say? On a separate sheet of paper, list five or six characteristics of the peanut that you might use to describe it.

Then, pick a number from 1 to 9. Now look at Figure A below and study the pictures of the peanut that corresponds to that number for thirty seconds. Concentrate only on that picture. Try not to look at the other pictures as you examine your peanut. Get to know your peanut as well as you can in the time allowed.

Figure A

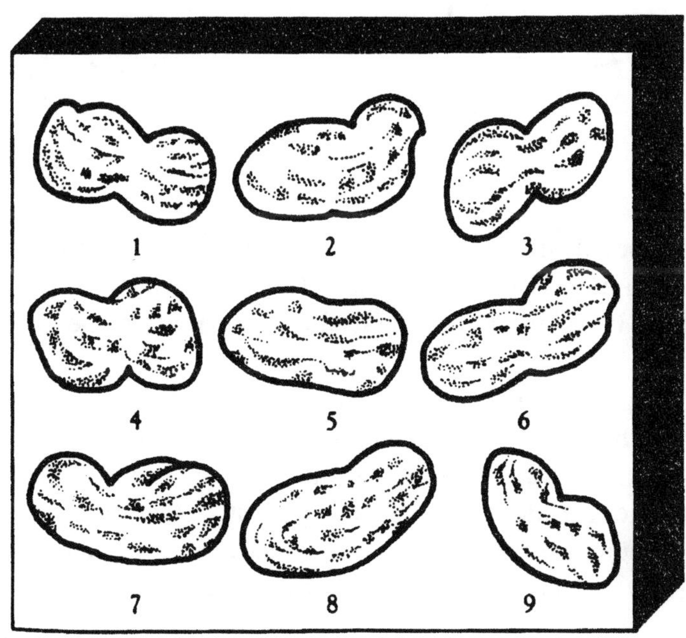

SOURCE: Reprinted by permission from page 135 of *Adjustment and Competence: Concepts & Applications* by Grasha and Kirschenbaum;

Look at Figure B and try to find your peanut *without looking at the picture of the peanut you selected in Figure A*. The pictures have been rearranged. Check the number of the picture in Figure B that you think corresponds to the peanut you studied with the correct answer given in the answer key.

Figure B

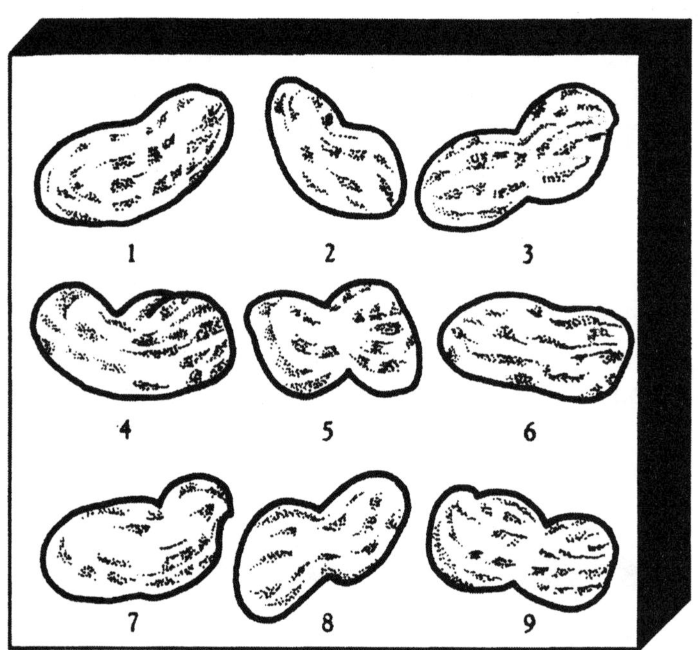

About 70 percent of the people doing this activity are able to find their peanut. Were you able to find your peanut? If you could find it, how helpful were the characteristics you listed earlier in assisting you to do this? If you were not able to find it, what are some of the reasons?

Most people doing this activity report that the characteristics they listed were not very helpful. What was useful were the individual characteristics of the peanuts. The fact that peanuts are "brown," "oval," "rough textured," "salty," or "used to make peanut butter" were generally unimportant characteristics for identifying a single peanut. When examined closely, each peanut is unique and most stereotypes of what "peanuts are really like" prove to be useless in identifying individual peanuts. Do you think that this is also true of people and other things that you might stereotype?

SCORING:

After selecting the number of the peanut in Figure 2 that you believe corresponds to the peanut you studied initially in Figure 1, check your responses below.

Original Position Figure 1	New Position Figure 2
1	8
2	9
3	6
4	7
5	4
6	5
7	2
8	3
9	1

Compare your scores with other people who have completed the same exercise. We have found that the average person gets about 4 correct. If you score 8 or more you have a bright future in any job that requires good observational powers.

I believe I have no prejudices whatsoever. All I need to know is that a man is a member of the human race. That's bad enough for me.

Mark Twain

It is well, when judging another, to remember that he is judging you with the same godlike and superior impartiality.

Arnold Bennett

13.3 THE CLASS PIE

"Groups" come in different sizes and different configurations. Almost any combination of people joined together for a purpose could be construed as a "group". One such "group" is your class. This exercise asks you to conceptualize your class as a group.

GOAL: To see your class as a small group and to analyze its structure.

DIRECTIONS: Imagine that the circle below is a pie representing the members of your class or discussion group, and divide the pie into slices (one per person). The size of each slice should indicate the amount of each person's contribution to the class. Be sure to include a slice for yourself and for your instructor, and identify each slice by the person's name or initials.

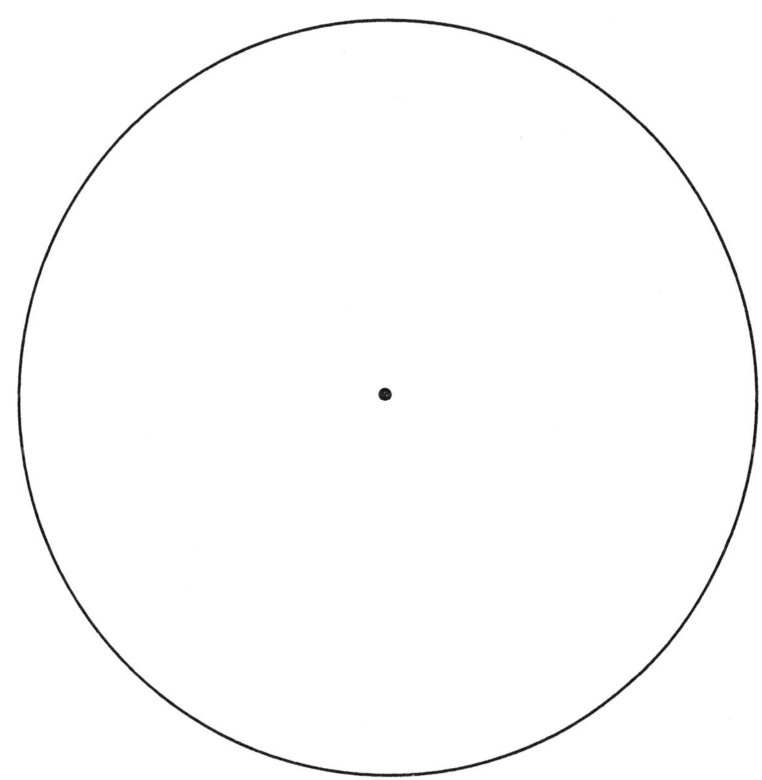

1. What criteria did you use to determine the amount of each person's contribution to the class (e.g., amount of talking, quality of comments, number of interesting questions, influence on others)?

2. Describe the way in which you divided the pie. That is, did you give everyone an equal slice, or did you give some people much larger slices than you gave to others?

3. Which three people received the biggest slices? Did they act as leaders of the group? If so, describe any aspects of their leadership behavior that differed from the behaviors listed in question 1.

4. How did you evaluate yourself in relation to the others in the group? What role did you play in the group? That is, how did you behave in class discussions?

13.4 GOOD AND BAD NEWS

There are many ways to assess the prevalence of prosocial or altruistic behaviors in a society, including direct observation and interviews. In a society that is so dependent on mass media, one very effective way to study the prevalence of prosocial behavior, compared with the prevalence of antisocial behavior, is to tabulate its coverage in the news media. This is an example of a *content analysis* in which you will be assigning each example to a category which are based upon criteria that may differ from one person to another, but among which there will be a lot of (validating) overlap in judgements between each person.

GOAL: To discover if there is a "slant" to the media coverage of news.

DIRECTIONS: Analyze the contents of your favorite television news program for a one week period, and record the number of prosocial and antisocial events that are reported, as well as the number of neutral events, on the following data sheet. Prosocial items would include acts of helping or kindness, awards, donations, and success stories. Antisocial news stories would include coverage of war, murder, rape, vandalism, and verbal attacks. Neutral news events would include stock market reports, weather forecasts, sports scores, announcements of new laws or food prices, and similar information. Specify the items in detail, especially those that do not obviously fit any of the categories, so that you can discuss them in class.

TV Station:______ Local or National News:________________

Neutral

____

MONDAY ____

Prosocial

____

____

Antisocial

____

SOURCE: Pines and Maslach, *Experiencing Social Psychology,* 3rd ed. Used with permission of McGraw Hill Inc. copyright 1992.

Neutral

TUESDAY

Prosocial

Antisocial

Neutral

WED.

Prosocial

Antisocial

Neutral

____

THURS. ______________________________

Prosocial

____

____

Antisocial

____

____

Neutral

____

FRIDAY ______________________________

Prosocial

____

____

Antisocial

____

____

1. How many prosocial events did you count? _____ Antisocial? _____ Neutral? _____

2. What do the results suggest?

3. Does the frequency of occurrence of prosocial events in the news truly reflect the frequency of the occurrence in real life?

13.5 RATE YOUR PREJUDICES

Prejudice is negative attitudes you hold towards the members of some group of people (or things for that matter, think of small children who won't eat any food because it is green), just because they are a member of that group. It is more than just racism. It's about how you treat unpopular people, or whether you're friends with a disabled person. How open is your mind? Let's look.

GOAL: To see if you have hidden prejudices.

DIRECTIONS: Complete the following sentences by choosing the statement you agree with most strongly.

1. People confined to wheelchairs...
   a. make me nervous.
   b. are completely helpless.
   c. deserve the same access to public facilities as everyone else.

2. Kids who grow up with a lot of money...
   a. are snobs.
   b. are self-destructive, and I feel sorry for them.
   c. are lucky they won't need financial aid in college.

3. Homeless people...
   a. are always looking for a handout.
   b. are unlucky victims of the American system.
   c. have gotten themselves into their bad situation.

4. When I'm in a room and someone tells an ethnic joke...
   a. that someone is usually me.
   b. I laugh out loud; I mean it's only a joke.
   c. I say, "That's not funny."

5. People who drive motorcycles...
   a. are naturally rebellious.
   b. save a lot of money on gas.
   c. like to drink and pick fights.

6. When I see someone wearing a crystal, I immediately think...
   a. they're easily led.
   b. they're pretty open-minded.
   c. they're completely wacko.

7. It seems to me that anyone who's fat...
   a. has no self-control
   b. doesn't fit in as well as everyone else.
   c. has something in common with Marlon Brando

8. People with AIDS...
   a. are sexually promiscuous.
   b. will likely die of this awful disease.
   c. got what they deserved.

9. Did you ever notice that people who live in small towns...
   a. are pretty unsophisticated.
   b. talk slower.
   c. are more likely to know their neighbors.

10. Blonds...
    a. are dumber than your average person.
    b. look really good with a tan.
    c. have a better chance at becoming a cheerleader.

11. In my opinion, old people...
    a. need other people to take care of them, and always tell the same stories over and over.
    b. are forgetful.
    c. have experienced a lot more than I have.

12. People who stutter...
    a. should not make broadcasting their career.
    b. are slightly retarded.
    c. are nervous a lot of the time.

13. The people in my school who consistently make the honor roll...
    a. always do their homework-even if "Melrose Place" is on.
    b. are insufferable nerds.
    c. don't have to be as nervous as everyone else about getting a good GPA.

14. People who wear black...
    a. are suicidal.
    b. are pretentious.
    c. like black.

15. If you're a jock...
    a. you're probably stupid.
    b. you're good at sports.
    c. you're treated like you're special at school.

16. Politicians...
    a. are all corrupt.
    b. don't care about the average person.
    c. are competitive.

17. All heavy metal chicks...
    a. listen to loud music.
    b. dress like slags.
    c. do drugs.

18. People who don't go to college...
    a. won't get anywhere in life.
    b. hate school.
    c. have other plans.

SCORING:

Use the following key to assign a point value to each of your answers then ad up the total number of points.

ITEM

1.	a.(1) b.(2) c.(0)		11.	a.(2)	b.(1)	c.(0)
2.	a.(2) b.(1) c.(0)		12.	a.(0)	b.(2)	c.(1)
3.	a.(2) b.(0) c.(1)		13.	a.(1)	b.(2)	c.(0)
4.	a.(2) b.(1) c.(0)		14.	a.(2)	b.(1)	c.(0)
5.	a.(1) b.(0) c.(2)		15.	a.(2)	b.(0)	c.(1)
6.	a.(1) b.(0) c.(2)		16.	a.(2)	b.(1)	c.(0)
7.	a.(2) b.(1) c.(0)		17.	a(0)	b.(1)	c.(2)
8.	a.(1) b.(0) c.(2)		18.	a(2)	b(1)	c(0)
9	a.(2) b.(1) c.(0)					
10.	a.(2) b.(0) c.(1)					

ANALYSIS:

Take Heed:

36-25: My oh, my. You've got a real problem. Your mind is so firmly shut that dynamite couldn't blast it open. You need to think about why you hold so many negative opinions about whole groups of people. Chances are it's because you don't know many people who aren't exactly like you, and it's about time you made a serious effort to meet some. Get a clue.

24-13: Everyone brings preconceptions to their daily interactions-it's just human. So don't exactly whip yourself to death for landing here. Still, you've got some consciousness-raising to do. Try to do a little self-education about the people you think are weird or different from you. Okay?

12-0: Well, aren't you the open-minded one! If you scored in this category, great. You're trying to be part of the solution, not the problem. And if you practice what you preach, we're doubly impressed.

14

SECTION FOURTEEN: STRESS AND HEALTH

The world is once again returning to the realization that the health of the body affects the mind and the health of the mind affects the body. Too much stress in either is harmful to both. Health psychology is the part of psychology that deals with the relationships between psychological variables and health.

All of the exercises in this section are designed to either identify or to diminish stress in your life. We recognize that college is a stressful time. We also know that some amount of stress is useful. With no stress, it would be unlikely that you would study for exams or even have purchased this book. Obviously, we are unable and unwilling to eliminate all stress from your life.

However, there are times when all of us are too stressful and we need ways to deal with it. The first exercise is a rather well known scale called the Social Readjustment Scale from Holmes and Rahe. This scale asks you to look at various life events as stressors to assess your level of stress. We added a few questions at the end (just to make the exercise more stressful.)

We then look at the phenomenon of "burn out". We modified this original work to substitute job stress for college stress. The final two exercises look at the second topic in this section, health. The first assesses mental health functioning. The second article is reprinted from *Shape Magazine* and looks at physical health and exercise.

As we said above, you will not be stress-free after this section. Nor should you want to be. But look at what you'll learn. First, you'll be introduced to a famous study by Holmes and Rahe. Then you'll get to read an article from a well known newspaper. Third, you'll assess your mental health competence. Finally, we introduce you to *Shape Magazine* to help you shape up.

Stress and Health exercises include:

14.1 The Social Readjustment Scale
14.2 Are You Burned Out?
14.3 Assessing How Well You Adapt
14.4 Finding The Fitness Balance In Your Life:
The Way To Win At Home

14.1 THE SOCIAL READJUSTMENT SCALE

There are two types of stressors in life. The first type consists of major event or crises. The second type is more insidious and is made up of minor daily hassles. Other exercises in the book looked at some of those. Now it is time to look at the really troublesome events in one's life.

GOAL: To help identify major stressors in your life.

DIRECTIONS: Think about the last six months of your life. On the table below, place a checkmark next to each of the events that you experienced during this period. Once you are done, add up the total number of Life Change Units that you have experienced.

Life Change Events

Family	**Life Change Units**
Death of a spouse	100
Divorce	73
Marital separation	65
Death of a close family member	63
Marriage	50
Marital reconciliation	45
Major changes in health of family	44
Pregnancy	40
Addition of new family member	39
Major change in arguments with spouse	35
Son or daughter leaving home	29
In-law troubles	29
Spouse starting or ending work	26
Major change in family get-togethers	15

Personal	**Life Change Units**
Detention in jail	63
Major personal injury or illness	53
Sexual difficulties	39
Death of a close friend	37
Outstanding personal achievement	28

SOURCE: The original list was reprinted from *The Journal of Psychosomatic Research*, Vol 11, pp 213-218, 1967 by Holmes and Rahe. Questions at end of exercise from Donovan & Rosato Copyright 1996.

Start or end formal schooling	26
Major change in living conditions	25
Major revision of personal habits	24
Changing to a new school	20
Change in residence	20
Major change in recreation	19
Major change in church activities	19
Major change in sleeping habits	16
Major change in eating habits	16
Vacation	13
Christmas	12
Minor violations of the law	11

Work	**Life Change Units**
Being fired from work	47
Retirement from work	45
Major business adjustment	39
Changing to different line of work	36
Major change in work responsibilities	26
Troubles with the boss	23
Major change in working conditions	20

SCORING:

Now add up your total points. There is no magical formula here. As we said before, it is not the event but rather how we evaluate it that truly determines the stressor. With that in mind, why not reassign points as the event might effect you. Start by assigning 100 to the worst thing you can imagine and work from there.

Add your new scores and compare with the previous list. Are you more or less stressed now? Were you surprised at any of the values in the original list? Do you agree that being fired is worth almost as many "points" as retirement? Does a spouse starting or ending work have the same impact? How about vacation as a stressor?

Note:

This book has been designed to appeal to individuals of various ages. As such, some of the exercises might have more relevance for one group than for another. This exercise might use examples of life situations for individuals who are attending college not immediately after high school. There are other similar scales for the more typically aged college student. The reader is invited to research such scales in the college library.

14.2 ARE YOU BURNED OUT?

Stress on a job (or at college) is often due to "burn out", essentially a form of frustration. The exercise which follows asks you to evaluate your present situation. Ideally this is designed for on the job feelings; however, since it is certainly possible to be burned out in school, please feel free to substitute "college" for work or job.

GOAL: To determine if you are (or if you have the potential to become) burned out.

DIRECTIONS: Rate each question according to the following scale:

1 - Never **2 - Rarely** **3 - Sometimes** **4 - Often** **5 - Always**

Do You:

Feel less competent or effective than you used to feel in your work?	1	2	3	4	5
Consider yourself unappreciated or "used"?	1	2	3	4	5
Dread going to work?	1	2	3	4	5
Feel overwhelmed in your work?	1	2	3	4	5
Feel your work is pointless or unimportant?	1	2	3	4	5
Watch the clock?	1	2	3	4	5
Avoid conversations with others (co-workers, customers, and supervisors in the work setting; family members at home)?	1	2	3	4	5
Rigidly apply rules without considering creative solutions?	1	2	3	4	5
Get frustrated by your work?	1	2	3	4	5

SOURCE: Reprinted with the permission of the *Washington Post*, 5 August, 1980, Section B page 5, "Careers: Confronting On The Job Burnout", by George Manning and Kent Curtis.

	1 - Never	2 - Rarely	3 - Sometimes	4 - Often	5 - Always
Miss work often?	1	2	3	4	5
Feel unchallenged by your work?	1	2	3	4	5
Does Your Work:					
Overload you?	1	2	3	4	5
Deny you rest periods, breaks, lunch time, sick leave, or vacation?	1	2	3	4	5
Pay too little?	1	2	3	4	5
Depend on uncertain funding sources?	1	2	3	4	5
Provide inadequate support to accomplish the job (budget, equipment, tools, people, etc.)?	1	2	3	4	5
Lack clear guidelines?	1	2	3	4	5
Entail so many different tasks that you feel fragmented?	1	2	3	4	5
Require you to deal with major or rapid changes?	1	2	3	4	5
Lack access to a social or professional support group?	1	2	3	4	5
Demand coping with a negative job image or angry people?	1	2	3	4	5
Depress you?	1	2	3	4	5

SCORING AND INTERPRETATION:

Add up your scores for the Up in Smoke test and insert your total:____

Scores	Category
94-110	Burnout
76- 93	Flame
58- 75	Smoke
40-57	Sparks
22-39	No Fire

Burnout: If your **score is between 94 and 110**, you are experiencing a very high level of stress in your work. Without some changes in yourself or your situation, your potential for stress-related illness is high. Consider seeking professional help for stress reduction and burnout prevention. Coping with stress at this level may also require help from others - supervisors, co-workers, and other associates at work, and spouse and other family members at home.

Flame: If you have **a score between 76 and 93**, you have a high amount of work-related stress and may have begun to burn out. Mark each question that you scored **4 or above**, and rank them in order of their effect on you, beginning with the ones that bother you the most. For at least your top three, evaluate what you can do to reduce the stress involved, and act to improve your attitude or situation. If your body is reflecting the stress, get a medical checkup.

Smoke: Scores between 58 and 75 represent a certain amount of stress in your work and are a sign that you have a fair chance of burning out unless you take corrective measures. For each question that scored **4 or above**, consider ways you can reduce the stress involved. As soon as possible, take action to improve your attitude or the situation surrounding those things that trouble you the most.

Sparks: If your **score is between 40 and 57**, you have a low amount of work-related stress and are unlikely to burn out. Look over those questions that you scored **3 or above**, and think about what you can do to reduce the stresses involved.

No Fire: People with **scores of 22 through 39** are mellow in their work, with almost no job-related stress. As long as they continue at this level, they are practically burnout-proof.

Nothing in life is to be feared,
it is only to be understood.
Marie Curie

The really happy person is one who can adapt and enjoy a change in the scenery when on a detour.
Unknown

14.3 ASSESSING HOW WELL YOU ADAPT

Competence refers to those behaviors that help us to meet the challenges of life creatively and to improve the quality of our lives. People demonstrate competence when their actions lead to growth- producing experiences. This can occur in several ways. Individuals may apply current skills in innovative ways, acquire new skills, or rearrange the environment to fit existing skills and abilities.

For example, a student with poor grades could exhibit competence by taking his current ability to read, to ask questions, and to answer questions and use them in an innovative fashion. He might combine them in the SQ3R method for studying. SQ3R stands for Survey, Question, Read, Recite, and Review information. It is a proven study aid that builds on existing basic abilities and often helps students improve their grades.

People who dislike their jobs might consider learning new skills or rearranging their environment to demonstrate competence. Acquiring more education and training is a good way to open up new job possibilities. Similarly, people can reshape the work environment by switching positions, creating a new position for themselves, or looking elsewhere for another place to work. Since the environment becomes more compatible with their skills and abilities, they are likely to enhance the overall quality of their lives.

We do not believe that people are "stuck" trying to adjust or trying to become competent. Both processes operate in life. Most of us use each of them at different times, and both are legitimate goals to pursue. You can decide whether "getting by," adequately handling a situation, or creatively coping is the strategy to choose. Depending upon how well you learn and apply the information presented, each way of meeting challenges is possible. After all, competence is accessible to us all and sometimes it is not even that difficult to experience, but we must be motivated and a bit creative in order to change our sometimes maladjusted, incompetent ways. An excellent place to begin is by identifying areas of your life where you could improve your current behaviors. Then, as you read the exercise, try to apply the principles presented to those areas.

GOAL: To help you begin the process of thinking about how you can improve your adaptation.

DIRECTIONS: Read each section and follow the instructions.

EXERCISE

Assessing How You Currently Adapt

Part I

How well do you think you currently adapt? It is difficult to answer this question without identifying how you behave in different situations. Below is a list of behaviors which help other people to adapt. Think of how you usually behave with your family, at school, at work, and in your social life. Place a check for each behavior that you feel you employ on a regular basis in each situation.

Checklist	Family	School	Work	Social Life
Seldom avoid problems	_____	_____	_____	_____
Ask for help when needed	_____	_____	_____	_____
Use time well	_____	_____	_____	_____
Set clear goals	_____	_____	_____	_____
Able to manage emotions	_____	_____	_____	_____
Ask for feedback	_____	_____	_____	_____
Use feedback from others	_____	_____	_____	_____
Anticipate future problems	_____	_____	_____	_____
Use good communication skills	_____	_____	_____	_____
Possess a sense of humor	_____	_____	_____	_____
Respond in a flexible manner	_____	_____	_____	_____
Work well with people	_____	_____	_____	_____
Able to learn from mistakes	_____	_____	_____	_____
Solve problems creatively	_____	_____	_____	_____
Try to improve skills	_____	_____	_____	_____
Display initiative	_____	_____	_____	_____
Take an interest in others	_____	_____	_____	_____
Accept responsibility	_____	_____	_____	_____

Checklist	Family	School	Work	Social Life
Able to meet personal needs	_____	_____	_____	_____
Take necessary risks	_____	_____	_____	_____
Have a positive outlook	_____	_____	_____	_____
Set reasonable goals	_____	_____	_____	_____
See problems as challenges	_____	_____	_____	_____
Know how to influence people	_____	_____	_____	_____
Able to manage conflict	_____	_____	_____	_____

Part II

The behaviors listed generally help people to adapt. Why were certain items absent in either your family, school, work, or social life? Do you believe that the absence of any item in the checklist contributes to any problems you experience in each setting? If you could do one thing tomorrow to make that item a part of your family, school, work, or social life, what would you do?

Would you describe your ability to adapt in each setting as adjusting or seeking competence? Perhaps you see yourself doing both. If so, which one tends to occur most often?

Exercise is bunk. If you are healthy, you don't need it;
if you are sick you shouldn't take it.
Henry Ford

Those who do not find the time for exercise
will have to find the time for illness.
Scotch Proverb

14.4 FINDING THE FITNESS BALANCE IN YOUR LIFE: THE WAY TO WIN AT HOME

An overwhelming fitness boom emerged in the '80s as the masses strived for perfectly formed and functioning bodies. People sought registered dietitians for nutritional guidance, personal trainers became the rage, and liposuction became an option when the rest seemed too difficult or too slow. Working out required belonging to the right club, diets became restrictive and confusing, and everything seemed to cause cancer.

The '90s offer an opportunity to define health and fitness in a broader context, in terms of a quality of life that requires balance. We still care about what we eat, but we also care about the impact of food packaging on the environment. We still need and want to exercise, but workouts must fit into our busy lifestyles and work with our family commitments. We'll no longer let our nutrition and fitness regiments be so controlling that they cause more stress than they relieve.

GOAL: To determine if you have a proper balance of fitness for your life.

DIRECTIONS: Ask yourself these questions to evaluate your success in balancing your life.

1. How often do you get vigorous, sustained aerobic exercise of at least 20 to 30 minutes per session?
    1. Four to five times a week
    2. Three times a week
    3. Once or twice a week
    4. Never - no regular exercise program

2. How often do you do strength-building and toning exercises such as sit-ups or push-ups, or use hand weights or weight-training equipment?
    1. More than twice a week
    2. Seldom
    3. Never

3. How often do you include stretching exercises and relaxation sessions in your fitness routine?
    1. More than three times a week
    2. Two to three times a week
    3. Seldom or once a week
    4. Never

4. Mark the response that best describes how you are coping with life.
   1. Seldom stressed, coping very well
   2. Sometimes stressed, coping fairly well
   3. Often stressed, difficulty coping
   4. Extremely stressed, unable to cope

5. Have you felt tired, worn out or exhausted during the past month?
   1. Seldom or never
   2. Only occasionally
   3. Less than half of the time
   4. The majority of the time

6. How often do you use drugs, alcohol or medications to help you relax or sleep?
   1. Never
   2. Rarely; a few times a year
   3. Sometimes; monthly
   4. Frequently; every week

7. How many caffeinated beverages do you usually drink per day?
   1. None
   2. One a day
   3. Two to three a day
   4. Four to five a day

8. In general, how strong is your social support with family and friends?
   1. Strong family/friend social support
   2. Some family/friend social support
   3. Little family/friend social support
   4. No close family/friend social support

9. How often do you eat a good breakfast (more than coffee and a sweet roll)?
   1. Always
   2. Usually
   3. Sporadically
   4. Seldom or never

10. How often do you allow time in your schedule for lunch?
    1. Always
    2. Usually
    3. Sporadically
    4. Seldom or never

11. Circle the type of snack food you usually eat between meals.
    1. Snack on fresh or dried fruit, whole-wheat crackers, vegetables or unbuttered air-popped popcorn
    2. Caffeinated beverages such as coffee or cola
    3. Candy, pastries, cookies, potato chips or fast foods

12. What kind of grains do you eat?
    1. Whole-wheat breads, whole-grain cereals (cooked or dry), brown rice
    2. A combination of whole-wheat and white bread and rolls, mostly whole-grain cereals
    3. Predominantly white bread and rolls, white rice and sweetened dry cereals
    4. Seldom eat bread, rice or cereal

13. Indicate the way you usually prepare food, or the type of food you like.
    High-fat: Frequently fry foods, use butter or shortening, creamy dressings.
    Lowfat: Usually broil, bake or poach, use vegetable oil or margarine sparingly, use lowfat dressing, avoid sauces.
    1. Food cooked primarily the lowfat way
    2. Food cooked both ways
    3. Food mostly cooked the high-fat way
    4. Food nearly always cooked the high-fat way

14. Indicate the type of meal you generally eat.
    1. Vegetarian diet, some fish or fowl, no red meat or predominantly fish or fowl, occasional lean cuts of red meat
    2. Regular mixed diet, including red meat
    3. Marbled cuts of red meat regularly

SCORING:

Add up the numbers of your answers in each section. (Answer 1 is worth 1 point; answer 2 is worth 2 points and so on.) Generally, the lower your score, the more healthful your lifestyle habits are. But we don't want you to concentrate on numbers here. Instead, if you find exercise is taking time from your relationship-building, or you're so busy at work you're forgetting to eat, try to get a little balance into your life. As you read the following exercise, check out the stress relief and nutrition guidelines to find out how you can make small changes that will really add up.

Above all, remember the 80/20 rule: If you eat well and exercise regularly 80 percent of the time, the 20 percent of the time when you're on vacation, or it's your birthday or you just don't feel like it, won't really matter. That's balance.

EXERCISE

Evaluate your exercise routine by looking at your responses to questions 1 through 3 in terms of the guidelines recommended below.

-) Do regular aerobic exercise in your target heart-rate range (70 to 85 percent of maximum) to elevate your metabolic rate, burn calories, promote cardiovascular fitness, relieve stress and promote HDL cholesterol production.

-) Aerobic exercise for 15 to 60 minutes, three to five times a week, is recommended for cardiovascular fitness.

-) Vary aerobic activities to use different muscle groups, prevent boredom and enhance long-term compliance. A menu of three or four aerobic activities to choose from also allows for seasonal activities and lets you work out around weather conditions.

-) For cardiovascular fitness, to reduce your risk of injury and to increase the likelihood you'll exercise regularly, plan longer, less intense workouts at your target heart rate on a consistent basis (four to five times a week), rather than shorter, more intense workouts.

-) Include strengthening exercises at least twice a week. Focus on upper body muscles with push-ups, weights, hand weights and/or resistant rubber bands. Include specific toning exercises such as crunches for the abdomen, leg lifts, squats and stepping for the thighs and buttocks.

15

SECTION FIFTEEN: PSYCHOLOGY IN THE WORKPLACE

We started this book by looking at what psychologists do. Throughout, we have given you exercises to either assess yourself or to provide you with (we hope) useful techniques. The final section is another application of what psychology is like. Recognizing how central work is to our lives, it is not surprising that psychologists turn their attention to the workplace. The focus this time is, therefore, psychology on the job.

The first exercise looks at how men and women differ in their communication styles on the job. The second exercise requires you to visit the office of three professors. This will help you to understand how office setup "communicates" to others. Finally, we give you an interest inventory from the U. S. Department of Labor. This could give you some insight into your perceived interests. (We couldn't end the book without using the "p" word one more time.)

What do you want to be when you grow up? By the end of this section, you may have a better idea. Perhaps this book and this course turned you on to psychology or to sociology. Whatever you eventually decide on, we are confident that psychology will be part of your workplace environment.

Psychology in the Workplace exercises include:

15.1 What's Your Gender Communication Quotient?
15.2 Professorial Environment
15.3 Career Interest Check List

15.1 WHAT'S YOUR GENDER COMMUNICATIONS QUOTIENT?

How much do you know about how men and women communicate with one another? The 20 items in this questionnaire are based on research conducted in classrooms, private homes, businesses, offices, hospitals-the places where people commonly work and socialize. The answers are at the end of the quiz.

GOAL: To determine gender differences in communications styles.

DIRECTIONS: Read each item and mark TRUE or FALSE as appropriate.

	TRUE	FALSE
1. Men talk more than women.	_____	_____
2. Men are more likely to interrupt women than they are to interrupt other men.	_____	_____
3. There are approximately ten times as many sexual terms for males as females in the English language.	_____	_____
4. During conversations, women spend more time gazing at their partner than do men.	_____	_____
5. Nonverbal messages carry more weight than verbal messages.	_____	_____
6. Female managers communicate with more emotional openness and drama than male managers.	_____	_____
7. Men not only control the content of conversations, but they also work harder in keeping conversations going.	_____	_____
8. When people hear generic words such as "mankind" and "he," they respond inclusively, indicating that the terms apply to both sexes.	_____	_____
9. Women are more likely to touch others than men are.	_____	_____
10. In classroom communications, male students receive more reprimands and criticism than female students.	_____	_____
11. Women are more likely than men to disclose information on intimate personal concerns.	_____	_____

Source: Reprinted with permission of the authors, John H. Gray and Hazel Rosema, University of Arkansas, Little Rock.

	TRUE	FALSE
12. Female speakers are more animated in their conversational style than are male speakers.	_____	_____
13. Women use less personal space than men.	_____	_____
14. When a male speaks, he is listened to more carefully than a female speaker, even when she makes the identical presentation.	_____	_____
15. In general, women speak in a more tentative style than do men.	_____	_____
16. Women are more likely to answer questions that are not addressed to them.	_____	_____
17. There is widespread sex segregation in schools, and it hinders effective classroom communication.	_____	_____
18. Female managers are seen by both male and female subordinates as better communicators than male managers.	_____	_____
19. In classroom communications, teachers are more likely to give verbal praise to females than to male students.	_____	_____
20. In general, men smile more often than women.	_____	_____

ANSWERS: True 1, 2, 4, 5, 10-15, 17, 18.

SCORING: (Donovan & Rosato)

10 or less correct: As the book is titled, Men are from Mars, Women are from Venus and you still think the Sun circles around the Earth. Run do not walk to the nearest source of training in understanding and communicating with the opposite gender.

11 to 15 correct: This is actually an average score. Of course when asked, over 90% of all people report being average. This is not bad but you still are leaving yourself open to a lot of unnecessary and even painful cross gender communication mistakes.

16+ correct: Unless you used to be a different gender at one time or another, you are a rare and sensitive individual to understand the differences in communication styles so well. Please have a long talk with those people who scored 10 or less.

John Gray is the author of the best selling book, "Men are From Mars, Women are From Venus." Gender psychologists and researchers (such as Deborah Tannen) are working hard to understand the various different gender subcultures and their communication "genderlects."

15.2 THE PROFESSORIAL ENVIRONMENT

How much does the physical layout of one's work environment influence the perception that others have of the person herself? This exercise looks at that issue.

The physical environment that surrounds a person can, without conscious intent or cognition, influence behavior and social interaction. Such things as the arrangement of furniture can encourage or discourage contact and intimacy and can indicate status differences (e.g. limiting the immediacy of contact is a very effective means of conveying high status). Thus, one professor's office may look cold and impersonal; whereas another's is friendly and casual, depending on furniture placement. In situations in which it is important to establish good rapport and intimacy, a seating arrangement which encourages immediacy is critical.

GOAL: To explore the relationship between the physical layout of various professors' offices and the general friendliness of those professors.

DIRECTIONS: First, establish criteria for evaluating the office environment and the professor's rapport with students. In evaluating the office environment, you might consider such variables as the placement of the desk (along the side of the wall or as a barrier between student and professor), the type and placement of chairs, and the amount of open space. In assessing the professor's rapport with students, you might consider such variables as availability (how many office hours the professor has and whether he or she is keeping them), the physical distance between student's and the professor's chairs, and the amount of eye contact between professor and student. Decide on five criteria for evaluating the office environment and five criteria for evaluating the professor's rapport with students, and list them on the data sheet. Then visit the office of three different professors (whom you have previously met) to talk about some topic of interest. Rate both the office and the professor's rapport with you according to your set of criteria.

DATA SHEET

VARIABLES TO BE USED	PROFESSOR A	PROFESSOR B	PROFESSOR C
ENVIRONMENT			
1.________	________	________	________
2.________	________	________	________
3.________	________	________	________
4.________	________	________	________
5.________	________	________	________
RAPPORT			
1.________	________	________	________
2.________	________	________	________
3.________	________	________	________
4.________	________	________	________
5.________	________	________	________

1. Look at the pattern of ratings and speculate on possible relationships between environment and behavior (e.g., how the placement of a desk can reduce personal contact).

2. Compare your criteria and your rating with those of other people in your class. What hypotheses do your collective ratings suggest?

3. According to your hypotheses, what would be the ideal office environment for promoting student-professor rapport? What would be the ideal environment for hindering it?

15.3 CAREER INTEREST CHECK LIST

Throughout this book, we have tried to give you a sense of what it would be like to work as a psychologist. For some of you, this will be your career path. Others will try to forget how to spell psychology. And some will end up with positions which are related to psychology. This last exercise will help you with that decision.

Below you will find activities listed in 23 distinct groups. Each group represents an occupational area (like forestry, or personal service); each activity within the group highlights a specific job function (like reporting the news, or playing games with children).

GOAL: To assist you in determining your vocational interest.

DIRECTIONS: Read each activity and mark those that you would like as jobs or hobbies. Be liberal in your marking. That is, mark it even if you are not totally infatuated with it and even if you think that you would like to try it. Conversely, if you have no interest in any of the activities in any group, please do not feel compelled to mark any. Finally, strike a balance between speed and thoughtfulness; do not dawdle but do not deliberate too long.

A

--- Sketching and painting portraits, landscapes, still life or figures on canvas.
--- Creating, designing and painting posters, signboards, showcards, charts, diagrams, labels, and illustrations for advertising copy, books, and magazines.
--- Modeling or carving various objects from wood, clay, plaster, or stone.
--- Sketching rooms and planning the arrangement of furniture, wall decorations, and color schemes.
--- Creating and drawing to scale patterns for new types and styles of clothes.

C

--- Writing magazine articles, plays, short stories, poems, or books.
--- Translating from one language to another.
--- Reporting news for a newspaper or magazine.
--- Writing or editing news items for a newspaper, periodical or book.
--- Doing literary research for historical publications.

(SOURCE: The Interest Check List is from the United States Department of Labor and is based upon categories from the *Dictionary of Occupational Titles* also published by that department. Interpretations by Donovan & Rosato,)

B

--- Playing a musical instrument.
--- Singing various types of songs.
--- Creating and composing musical compositions or arranging a melody for orchestral use.
--- Conducting an orchestra.
--- Studying musical theory and techniques, melody, and harmony.

D

--- Acting in play/drama production.
--- Announcing radio programs.
--- Dancing for the entertainment of others.
--- Making a living by playing football, baseball, hockey or other sports.
--- Entertaining others by juggling, sleight-of-hand, pantomime, or magic

E

--- Developing advertising campaigns.
--- Applying the principles of accounting, statistical analysis, contracts, credit, markeying conditions, and applied psychology to the problems of business.
--- Drawing up legal documents such as contracts, partnerships, deeds, and wills.
--- Conducting lawsuits.
--- Working up sales methods.

F

--- Figuring out arithmetic problems using multiplication, division, squares, and square roots.
--- Copying long lists of numbers and checking to be sure they are copied right.
--- Finding mistakes in answers to arithmetic problems.
--- Doing addition and subtraction.
--- Working with fractions and decimals.

G

--- Keeping business records, such as sales slips, receipts, bills, attendance records, and amount of goods purchased or work done.
--- Typing letters and reports.
--- Taking dictation in shorthand or on a stenotype machine.

I

--- Teaching school.
--- Talking to individuals or couples and assisting them in solving their personal or fin- problems.
--- Interviewing and advising individuals concerning their schooling, jobs, and social problems.
--- Studying social and economic conditions in order to help individuals or groups solve problems of general welfare.
--- Enforcing laws involving fire and crime prevention, traffic, sanitation, or immigration.

J

--- Planning a balanced diet (planning a menu or a meal).
--- Mixing foods to obtain new flavor.
--- Going to some trouble to make foods look attractive.
--- Learning the right way to season foods.
--- Selecting meats and vegetables in a grocery store for

--- Receiving, checking, counting, grading, examining, and storing supplies.
--- Sorting, indexing, and assembling papers and other written records.

H

--- Being a salesclerk, selling or taking tickets, handling money, or making change.
--- Answering the telephone.
--- Giving people information such as street directions or location of merchandise in stores.
--- Preparing lists of prospects and contacting them in order to make sales.
--- Attempting to interest prospective buyers by showing sample articles or displaying a catalog.

freshness and quality.

K

--- Playing games with children.
--- Telling stories to children.
--- Looking after children to see that they are kept neat and clean.
--- Taking care of children when they are sick.
--- Helping children dress or undress.

L

--- Giving first aid treatment.
--- Setting tables and serving food or drinks.
--- Acting as a hostess or headwaiter in a dining room.
--- Caring for people's hair and fixing their nails.
--- Waiting on other people and caring for their clothes.

M

--- Studying the soils, weather, climate, and so on in which plants and animals live and grow best.
--- Plowing, planting, cultivating, or harvesting crops.
--- Trying out various methods of growing plants to find the best way.
--- Breeding, raising, and caring for livestock such as cattle, sheep, hogs, and chickens.

N

--- Catching fish with nets, hooks, harpoons, spears, or guns.
--- Cleaning fish.
--- Steering ships and plotting a course with the aid of a compass or sextant.

P

--- Designing machinery and mechanical or electrical equipment.
--- Developing and executing plans for the construction of buildings or bridges.
--- Using drafting tools to prepare detailed plans and drawings for buildings or machines.
--- Doing research in a chemical, physical, or biological laboratory.
--- Drawing maps.

Q

--- Taking apart mechanical things such as bicycles, automobile engines, pumps, typewriters, or guns and putting them back together again.
--- Examining mechanical equipment for wear or damaged parts to see what

--- Standing watch on a ship to look out for rocks, lighthouses, buoys, or other ships.
--- Observing activity of fish to determine their habits and food requirements.

O

--- Using a trap to catch animals.
--- Acting as a guide for hunting parties.
--- Chopping or sawing down trees and trimming branches from trees using an ax or saw.
--- Moving or piling up stacks of logs and loading and fastening logs with chains.
--- Caring for forests by looking out for fires or tree diseases.

needs to be done.
--- Following complicated directions and diagrams to put parts of machines together.
--- Tuning up motors to see that they are running right.
--- Greasing and oiling machines.

R

--- Repairing electric stoves, refrigerators, vacuum cleaners, fans, and motors.
--- Studying the theory of electricity, including direct and alternating current, volts, amperes, ohms, etc.
--- Wiring, splicing, soldering, and insulating electrical connections.
--- Building and testing radio sets.
--- Changing fuses, repairing electric irons, wiring lamps, fixing light plugs and short circuits.

S

--- Working on scaffolds and climbing around on buildings while assembling large pieces with a hammer, rivets, or welding equipment.
--- Painting, plastering, puttying, or paper-hanging.
--- Working with hand tools such as saws, plumb lines, rulers, and squares.
--- Bending, threading, and fitting pipes, fixing drains and faucets.
--- Doing carpentry, plumbing, floor-laying, or roofing.

U

--- Running lathes, drill presses, and other machine shop equipment.
--- Making calculations to determine angles, curves, or shapes of small metal or wooden parts.
--- Pushing levers and buttons or turning handwheels to start, stop, slow down or speed up machines.
--- Operating heavy equipment to move dirt or rocks.
--- Making parts and tools from metal.

V

--- Doing freehand lettering or copying sketches on wood, metal, canvas, or film.
--- Making photographic copies of drawings, re-

T

--- Assembling or repairing instruments such as watches, locks, cameras, fountain pens, or field glasses.
--- Examining, inspecting, and separating objects according to quality, size, color, or weight.
--- Cutting and shaping glass or stone for jewelry and similar small articles.
--- Cutting, shaping, and rolling dough for breads and pastries.
--- Cutting, sewing, or repairing clothing, shoes, or other articles from cloth, leather, or fur.

W

--- Observing formulas, timing, temperature, and pressure directions.
--- Handling ore pouring hot metals, or plating metals.
--- Operating furnaces, boilers, ovens, and other equipment.
--- Grinding, mixing, or separating chemicals.
--- Measuring, mixing, or cooking foods for canning.

cords, or pictures for books or newspapers.
--- Setting type by hand or machine for printing, or working with sizes, styles, and spacing of type or proofreading.
--- Using soft crayon to copy maps, charts, posters, and drawings.
--- Cutting designs or letters into metal, stone, or glass, using hand tools or engraving wheels.

SCORING:

First add up the number of marks you placed in each group of activities and record them below:

A___ B___ C___ D___ E___ F___ G___ H___ I___ J___ K___

L___ M___ N___ O___ P___ Q___ R___ S___ T___ U___ V___

W___

INTERPRETING YOUR SCORES

The letters listed below are adjacent to the occupational group which they represent:

A Artistic
B Musical
C Literary
D Entertainment
E Clerical and Sales: Technical Work
F Clerical and Sales: Computing Work
G Recording and General Clerical Work
H Public Contract Work
I Service Work: Public Service
J Service Work: Cooking
K Child Care
L Personal Service
M Farming
N Marine
O Forestry
P Engineering: Technical Work
Q Mechanical Work
R Electrical Work
S Structural Crafts
T Bench Crafts
U Machinery and Machine Operating
V Graphic Art Work
W Processing

List the letters of the four groups which have the **highest** number of marks on the lines below.

___ ____

___ ____

___ ____

___ ____

Now do the same for the four **lowest** numbers of marks.

___ ____

___ ____

___ ____

___ ____

ABOUT INTEREST INVENTORIES

One might ask why interest inventories are necessary. There are a number of reasons. One is that results from the individual can be compared with the results from a large group. The assumption is that if Person A is employed in Occupational Area A and **enjoys** it, then someone with similar interests would enjoy that occupation also. Inventories spark interests in areas (or kill the spark) by specifying activities required in the occupation.

How stable are interests? It depends. (Did you really expect any other answer from a psychologist?) First, interests are highly unstable through adolescence. Second, in more recent years, the instability has expanded into later years (the stability of interests cannot be established until most people are in their late 20's). Finally, stability is related to educational level. More highly educated people have less stable interests than less formally educated people. Can you guess why?...Well, perhaps it is because the former group has more options and can therefore change jobs more readily than the latter.

Finally, the point must be made that **interest does not equal aptitude.** Having an interest in an area does not mean that one would be successful at it. Actually a better way to view the interest/aptitude relationship is to reverse it. It is much more likely that **ability leads to interest.** Most of us tend to enjoy what we are good at because we experience success when we attempt it. We also lose interest quickly when we are unsuccessful at a task.

LAST WORDS

Our hope is that this book and the exercises herein, has provided you with some insight into yourself, into the role of psychologist, and perhaps opened your eyes to other related (and not so related) occupational areas. We also hope that you enjoyed completing these exercises as much we did in gathering and developing them. We look forward to your comments and contributions which will go into improving and enhancing the 2nd edition of *Psychologically Speaking*.

TO BOLDLY GO

Some of you who have made it through to this point may be interested in learning more about psychology as a career and profession. Two groups exist who can help you with this, the American Psychological Association (APA) and the Canadian Psychological Association (CPA). Both groups publish several items about psychology and becoming a psychologist. They also support and encourage student membership in the organizations.

You can (and should) become a student member of these groups. You can join the APA for only $25 per year for which you receive the Monitor, the APA's monthly newsletter, the American Psychologist, its' official journal, discounts on books and journals published by the APA. You also get the chance to link up to various specialty areas within psychology where you can be in direct touch with what is going on in your particular fields of interest. You can join the CPA for $10. Their addresses are, The American Psychological Association, 750 First Street, N.E., Washington D.C., 2002 and, The Canadian Psychological Association, Vincent Road, Old Chelsea, Quebec, J0X 2N0.

To help you in your quest, the following four items are published by the APA:

(1) **Careers in Psychology**. This 28 page booklet outlines the many fields in which professional psychologists work with information about each. Students can receive a free single copy.

(2) **Is Psychology the Major for You?** This book is more detailed than the above and is written to guide the psychology major from student to career. Its' 137 pages provides you with a complete introduction to different psychology careers, how to find a job in the field, and how to utilize career counseling.

(3) **Preparing for Graduate Study in Psychology: NOT for Seniors Only!** is a 96 page manual to planning out your campaign to a successful admission to a graduate program in psychology. It includes preparation for students who may not have all the requirements quite yet. It takes you from what courses you'll need through acquiring recommendations, preparing resumes, completing applications and practicing interviews.

(4) **Graduate Study in Psychology and Associated Fields** is a comprehensive 600 page guide to all graduate psychology programs in the U.S. and Canada. It is the reference to help you compare and evaluate the various programs available to you. It lists the various specialities offered at each program, admission requirements, housing and assistance, tuition and other need to know materials.

The CPA publishes:

(1) **The Graduate Guide: Descriptions of Graduate Psychology Programs in Canadian Universities.**

Ciao!